Macbeth

William Shakespeare

Guide written and developed by
John Mahoney and Stewart Martin

Charles Letts & Co Ltd
London, Edinburgh & New York

First published 1987
by Charles Letts & Co Ltd
Diary House, Borough Road, London SE1 1DW
Reprinted 1988

Illustration: Peter McClure

Stewart Martin is an Honours graduate of Lancaster University, where he read English
and Sociology. He has worked both in the UK and abroad as a writer, a teacher, and an
educational consultant. He is married with three children, and is currently deputy
headmaster at Ossett School in West Yorkshire.

John Mahoney has taught English for twenty years. He has been head of English
department in three schools and has wide experience of preparing students at all levels
for most examination boards. He has worked both in the UK and North America
producing educational books and computer software on English language and literature.
He is married with three children and lives in Worcestershire.

British Library Cataloguing in Publication Data
　　Mahoney, John
　　Macbeth: William Shakespeare: guide
　　(Guides to literature)
　　1. Shakespeare, William. Macbeth
　　I. Title
　　II. Martin, Stewart   III. Series 822.3'3
　　PR2823

ISBN 0 85097 767 3

Printed and bound in Great Britain by
Charles Letts (Scotland) Ltd

Contents

	Page
To the student	5
William Shakespeare	6
Map of place-names	8
Understanding *Macbeth* *(An exploration of the major topics and themes in this play.)*	10
Analysis chart *(This shows important events, where they happen, time sequence, characters, and where to find them in the text and this guide.)*	14
Finding your way around the commentary	16
Commentary	19
Characters in the play	65
What happens in each act	67
Coursework and preparing for the examination	71
Studying the text	71
Writing the essay	72
Sitting the examination	74
Glossary of literary terms	77

To the student

This study companion to your English literature text acts as a guide to the novel or play being studied. It suggests ways in which you can explore content and context, and focuses your attention on those matters which will lead to an understanding, appreciative and sensitive response to the work of literature being studied.

Whilst covering all those aspects dealt with in the traditional-style study aid, more importantly, it is a flexible companion to study, enabling you to organize the patterns of study and priorities which reflect your particular needs at any given moment.

Whilst in many places descriptive, it is never prescriptive, always encouraging a sensitive personal response to a work of literature, rather than the shallow repetition of others' opinions. Such objectives have always been those of the good teacher, and have always assisted the student to gain high grades in 16+ examinations in English literature. These same factors are also relevant to students who are doing coursework in English literature for the purposes of continual assessment.

The major part of this guide is the 'Commentary' where you will find a detailed commentary and analysis of all the important things you should know and study for your examination. There is also a section giving practical help on how to study a set text, write the type of essay that will gain high marks, prepare coursework and a guide to sitting examinations.

Used sensibly, this guide will be invaluable in your studies and help ensure your success in the course.

With Shakespearian plays there are variations in the text from edition to edition. However, any edition of *Macbeth* can be used with this guide if you refer to the actual quotation line rather than to the act, scene and line reference.

William Shakespeare

Not much is known for certain about Shakespeare's private life and it matters little for an enjoyment of his plays. We know that he was born in 1564 and brought up in Stratford-on-Avon, that he went to London in 1586, wrote poetry, acted in the theatre and was co-author of some plays. He seems to have started writing plays under his own name in about 1591. He was a prolific writer, and within two or three years he produced several comedies and histories, as well as a sort of horror tragedy. Compared with the work of previous playwrights these early plays were outstanding for their style and characterization, but for Shakespeare they were merely an apprenticeship for his later work. He died in 1616.

Most of the Comedies and Histories were written between 1590 and 1600, but between 1601 and 1606 appeared the four great Tragedies, of which *Macbeth* is the last, the others being *Hamlet*, *Othello* and *King Lear*. All these revolve round a person of social or intellectual status whose life is ruined by one great mistake or character flaw. Shakespeare had already developed his great gift for dramatic characterization but these four plays reveal a brilliant mastery of poetic image.

The political and social background to Macbeth

Shakespeare was not an especially 'political' writer. The social and political comment which we can identify in his plays tends simply to reflect the accepted ideas of his time, so we need to understand these. The Tudors had made the Crown safer than ever before and secured a comparatively trouble-free aristocracy and peasant class. Yet the rising middle class, and the new working class of the town, were exerting more influence and demanding more social, religious and economic freedom than the established order could cope with all at once. Although times were obviously changing, there was the constant necessity to reinforce the idea of a framework of order essential to the well-being of the State.

There was a natural order in the universe according to Elizabethan philosophy, ordained by God, headed on earth by the King (the Lord's anointed) and in which everybody had an appointed place. God or the King could raise individuals or lower them but any attempt on the individual's part to control or change the natural order would result in confusion and chaos. So we see in *Macbeth* great emphasis on the virtue of order and formality, on the sanctity of the Crown, and on the acceptance of fate and the future, and this emphasis can be felt in both theme and imagery. Once this order has been broken (in this play through the murder of a rightful monarch) chaos ensues and the associated imagery is of fear, sickness, decay, blood and storm.

Macbeth also reflects the beliefs and preoccupations of James I, the king at the time for whom it was probably first performed. James I had been on the throne for three years. He had united the kingdoms of England and Scotland and the Crown seemed more secure than ever. Notice how the future monarch envisaged in *Macbeth* was to be a combination of the virtuous qualities of Banquo from whom the Scottish kings were to descend, and the holy powers of the English king who could heal the sick; James I was descended from both these lines. (Shakespeare was obviously an astute watcher of politics!) Over the previous two centuries the theory that kings were appointed by God and succeeded through heredity had been established, and one of its chief exponents was James I. (In *Macbeth* the next legal monarch has to be Duncan's son, although this is probably not true historically.) Early in his reign, James began to persecute religious extremists, such as the Puritans and Jesuits; one outcome of this was the Gunpowder Plot of 1605, said to be Jesuit-inspired. (The 'equivocation' or false swearing of one of the conspirators at his trial is lampooned by the Porter in *Macbeth*.)

The dramatic sources of Macbeth

The basic plot of the play was taken from Holinshed's *Chronicles* and probably other sources as well. It is possible that an earlier playwright has also used the subject. If you seek out those sources that still exist you will find an enormous gulf between them and Shakespeare's play. Shakespeare did not *copy* the *Chronicles* but only took the idea and then changed characters, introduced new characters, new scenes and new ideas; he also gives us insights into the mind and motives of not only Macbeth but also Lady Macbeth.

The ghost of Banquo is Shakespeare's invention, but here we may see another influence at work. Contemporary audiences were fond of scary manifestations of witches, ghosts and mad people. James I had himself written about witches, and supernatural creatures are certainly mentioned in the play's sources. However, it would be naïve to dismiss these as contemporary devices of no relevance to our time. Shakespeare's Witches are the literal embodiment of evil; we may see them as the subconscious temptation to do what we know is wrong. Coming to terms with such urges is part of our own morality.

It does not matter whether a ghost can actually be seen on stage or not, since we may recognize that the ghost is a symbol of Macbeth's horror and guilt at what he has done. Psychological illness following the suppression of guilt feelings might be better documented these days, but it is no better observed than it was by Shakespeare in his portrayal of Lady Macbeth in the sleep-walking scene. One of the things which makes Shakespeare unique is his wonderful understanding of the human mind, his sympathy with the individual faced with the pressures of society and the overpowering vastness of the greater world outside, as well as his ability to help us understand these things by the power of his language.

ORKNEY

The Western Isles

CAITHNESS

SUTHERLAND

NORDREYS

Routes of
the Norse Invaders

ROSS

Moray Firth

Forres
Cawdor
Inverness

MORAY

CALEDONIA

North

Sea

ALBAN

Firth of Tay

FIFE

Port of
Menteith

Firth of Forth

Stirling

Iona

MULL

AlcLyde
Renfrew

holyrood

Lindisfarne
(holy Island)

Colne-kill

SUDREYS

LOTHIAN

Melrose   Kelso
Selkirk

Strathclyde

BERNICIA

Cumberland

Northumberla

IRELAND

GALLOWAY

English miles

0   10   20   30

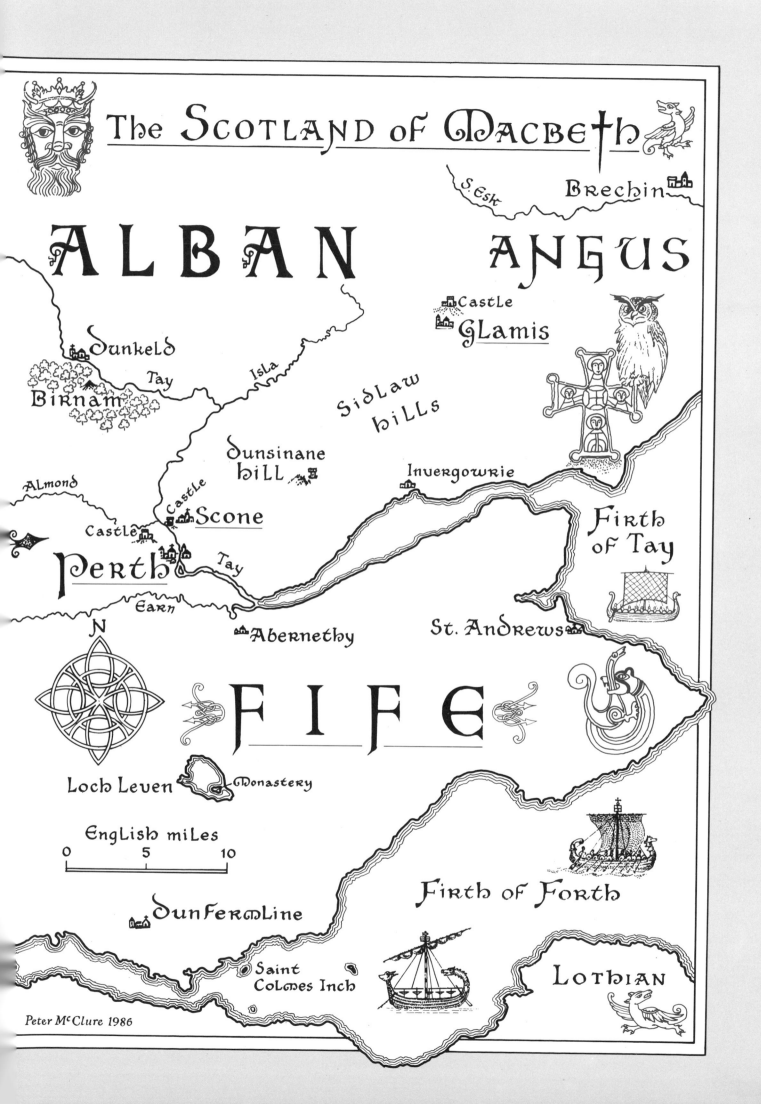

The Scotland of Macbeth

S. Esk

Brechin

ALBAN

ANGUS

Castle
Glamis

Dunkeld

Tay

Isla

Birnam

Sidlaw hills

Dunsinane hill

Invergowrie

Almond

Castle

Scone

Firth
of Tay

Castle

Perth

Tay

Earn

N

Abernethy

St. Andrews

FIFE

Loch Leven

Monastery

English miles

0   5   10

Dunfermline

Firth of Forth

Saint
Colmes Inch

LOTHIAN

Peter Mc Clure 1986

Understanding Macbeth
An exploration of the major topics and themes in the play

Summary of themes

Ambition

Both Macbeth and Lady Macbeth are ambitious, but Lady Macbeth is single-minded whereas Macbeth originally has scruples. These are overcome by the Witches and Lady Macbeth and he murders to achieve his ambition. It gives him no satisfaction; he cannot command loyalty, only fear, and he loses everything. We are encouraged to see that ambition should only be realized through ability or good fortune, otherwise it is doomed to eventual disaster.

Animals

Animals are part of the Elizabethan 'natural order' of the universe and are sometimes seen as parallels of the character and moods of the human race. The animal imagery in the play makes these connections. For example, we see how Lady Macbeth thinks of the croaking raven, Banquo the paternal martlet. Birds of prey and ill-omens abound in the animal imagery of the play: toads and snakes suit the Witches; Macbeth was a lion but eventually becomes a helpless bear.

Aspects of style

Shakespeare takes an old legend and creates a work of art. How he does this is a part of his genius which we can begin to comprehend by studying his power of characterization, imagery and, above all, his skill at interweaving characters and settings, of speeding or slowing down the pace and generally shaping a satisfactory whole. Wherever particularly interesting examples of these occur they will be mentioned in the commentary. For example, we can learn about a character by what he says and does, but a soliloquy, in which the character talks to himself and the audience overhears, is the means whereby we can understand his thoughts and motives. Untroubled characters have little need of soliloquy because they are what they seem – they have nothing to hide. A close study of all the soliloquies is essential to the clear understanding of the leading characters in the play.

Banquet

The theme of order is echoed in the imagery of the banquet. Macbeth's good qualities are a banquet to Duncan; Macbeth sees sleep as part of nature's banquet. But Macbeth's royal banquet is disrupted by his own fear and guilt. At the end of the play he has 'supped full with horrors', and order has become chaos. Eating and food are seen as parallels to the idea of nourishment in general: sleep nourishes the weary, order and calm nourish civilized society, and so on.

Blood

From the beginning of the play, when Macbeth is described as bathing 'in reeking wounds', blood becomes a recurring image. Lady Macbeth asks the spirits to 'Make thick my blood'; Macbeth's fear is that 'blood will have blood'. Other allusions impress upon us that this is what tyranny comes down to – bloodshed.

Chaos

An atmosphere of chaos introduces the play, with the Witches' 'Fair is foul, and foul is fair', a confusing paradox. The Witches confuse Macbeth; they 'cannot be ill, cannot be good'. Confusion reigns in nature before the murder, and Macbeth's banquet is chaotic.

Morality is turned upside down when

> 'to do harm
> Is often laudable, to do good sometime
> Accounted dangerous folly'
> (Lady Macduff)

Order only returns with Malcolm. The Elizabethans saw chaos as something which was kept at bay in the world only by the actions of men. It was seen as something actively trying to assert its influence all the time – like the powers of darkness and evil, but not the same as them.

Children

The imagery of the helplessness and innocence of children contrasts painfully with Macbeth's hatred of Banquo's children, his attempted murder of Fleance ('the worm') and his successful murder of Macduff's children. Macbeth likens pity to 'a naked new-born babe', but he has no pity, and will kill the babe. Children are used in the apparitions to show both the innocence and the potential of human beings. This is why Macbeth fears children, because of what they may imply about an unknown future. This is also why Macbeth desires so strongly to know the future from the Witches.

Clothing

If you take over another actor's part in a play, his costume probably won't fit you and may hinder your performance. The robes of kingship hinder Macbeth; they eventually come to symbolize his unsuitability for the role he has assumed, since he has taken over a role which rightly belongs to another. The idea of 'borrowed robes' is constantly present, and Macbeth's impatience to get back into his accustomed armour at the end of the play is his desperate attempt to return to his natural station. Similarly, we see many references to the uses of clothing, such as 'cloaking', 'wrapt' and so on.

The Crown

The Crown represents not only the Head of State but the head of the natural order. Since the King is the 'Lord's anointed' and his successor must be descended in blood from him, the authority of the Crown involves the powers of both God and nature, so any assault on it is both blasphemous and unnatural. In *Macbeth* the Crown's true heirs are virtuous, even saintly, whereas Macbeth is vicious and immoral.

Darkness

Macbeth says to the stars 'hide your fires'. Lady Macbeth wants the night to be covered 'by the dunnest smoke of hell'. Evil is best performed at night and throughout the play images of darkness add to the atmosphere of evil and confusion. Darkness is seen as an active force in nature and in the minds of people, and often the natural world echoes the emotional or mental state of the key characters through the weather, the time of day or the actions of animals. Sometimes these devices are also used to prepare us for the coming of evil deeds.

Dreams

Macbeth is tormented by dreams and visions. Obsessed as he is, his grasp on reality is tenuous. Banquo dreams at night of the Witches, but his days are clear; Macbeth on the other hand has a waking vision of 'a dagger of the mind' and of 'gory locks'. How 'real' are the Apparitions? Is Macbeth's cry of 'no more sights!' an expression of the fear of a guilty man? Dreams are not necessarily seen as a natural part of sleep, which is why they are treated separately here. Sleep is seen as being concerned with the idea of nourishment (see 'Banquet' on p10) and dreams are depicted as disturbances in this process, as being unpleasant and often ominous.

Fate

Fate is seen by all the play's characters, except Macbeth, as something unpredictable and uncontrollable, for example as a 'rebel's whore' when allowing the apparent success of the faction against Duncan at the start of the play. Encouraged by the Witches, Macbeth thinks that fate is on his side, and later that he can actually control it. Macbeth asks fate to come 'into the list' on his side; but even the Witches cannot control fate, only prophesy it.

Fear

Those with a clear conscience do not feel fear, except when it is evoked by natural suspicions. Duncan has 'absolute trust' in the Thane of Cawdor. Macbeth, on the other hand, is afraid even of his own thoughts after he meets the Witches, and after Duncan's death fear permeates the play, and reaches Ross, Lady Macduff, Malcolm and Macduff. Macbeth only loses his fear when he meets his soldier's death. Notice that Macbeth is not afraid of *physical* danger.

Growth

The natural order is symbolized in images of growth. But weeds as well as useful plants can grow, and ideas can germinate too. Duncan 'plants' Macbeth when he honours him. The 'seeds of time' and the 'seeds of Banquo' fascinate Macbeth. Under Macbeth Scotland becomes 'drowned with weeds' but Malcolm will 'plant newly'. Growth is linked with the theme and imagery of children in the play.

Haste

Haste is associated with Macbeth and the urgency of his ambition. Duncan's 'swiftest wing of recompense is slow to overtake thee' must become literally true. Images of speed, like the spur and 'vaulting ambition', emphasize this. Macbeth causes others to rush to escape him; Macduff has to 'fly the land'. Macbeth cannot bear waiting, uncertainty and inaction – for instance, look at how keen he is to don armour at the end of the play.

Light

Light imagery is associated with innocence and purity. To Duncan signs of nobleness are 'like stars', and Macbeth realizes that Duncan is 'clear in his great office'. Macbeth and Lady Macbeth fear and avoid the light because it will show up their guilt, but Lady Macbeth, when mad with guilt, has a 'light by her continually'. Light is associated with truth, openness and goodness.

Loyalty

The idea of loyalty in *Macbeth* is linked with the concepts of order, the Crown and the State, which all depend on the unswerving loyalty of the King's subjects, which is a moral duty rather than a personal choice. Macduff and Macolm remain loyal to the dead King and survive; Lennox and Ross switch loyalties just in time. Banquo unwisely places his personal loyalty to Macbeth above the higher loyalty, and is killed. Macbeth's failure in the end shows that nobody can gain from disloyalty.

Noise

Everything about Macbeth is associated with noise. His first appearance is to the sound of a drum. He fears that Duncan's virtues will be 'trumpet-tongued'. Macbeth's crimes, according to Macduff, make heaven resound. Howling and shrieking form the background to Macbeth's actions. Order creates peace, disorder creates noise.

Order

Order is an important theme in the play, since it is the disruption of order which is Macbeth's main crime. The idea of order embraces both the natural order and the order of the State; these are linked because the divinely-appointed king is at the head of the natural order of humanity where all people know their place. The moral and religious code of the time, then as now, supported the order of the State. Macbeth upsets every kind of order; political, social, domestic, family, and even 'mental' order and stability.

Portents

In Shakespeare's as in Roman times portents were considered to be omens of amazing or 'unnatural' events, the actual events themselves being unpredictable. Portents of evil abound before and during Duncan's murder, starting with the presence of the Witches. In *Macbeth* the audience often knows what mischief is afoot when some of the characters do not, so portents can be a form of dramatic irony. Note that unnatural happenings are in themselves portents of the upset of the natural order, which leads to chaos.

Prophecy

The Witches' prophecies are an important part of the plot, but to understand their significance one needs to know that in Shakespeare's time prophecy was considered to be an actual 'gift', either from God or from the Devil. Banquo regards the Witches as 'instruments of darkness'; Macbeth's fatal mistake was that he believed them–because he wanted to. By contrast the English King has 'a heavenly gift of prophecy'.

Sickness

As chaos follows disturbance of the State, so sickness follows disturbance of the body or mind, and we are continually meeting these complementary images of physical and mental disorder. Macbeth's brain is 'heat-oppressed'; he wears his 'health but sickly' for fear of Banquo. Lady Macbeth says things are 'without all remedy' and Macduff looks forward to the 'wholesome days' in Scotland when tyranny is defeated. Lady Macbeth's eventual illness is seen as a criticism of her spiritual and moral disorder.

Sleep

Sleep is natural and the ability to sleep is associated with being innocent. Macbeth's actions go against nature itself. Horrified after Duncan's death, he feels he has murdered sleep, nature's own gift. Malcolm's sleep is 'downy' but Macbeth is punished by sleeplessness, and Lady Macbeth relives the murder in her sleep.

The State

The Tudors had worked hard to establish in the minds of common folk the idea that loyalty was owed to the State and not to some local feudal lord. In Act One, the Thane of Cawdor's crime was to fight against the State; Macbeth fought for it and was a hero. The Crown is the head of the State as well as of the natural order, so the murder of a king is an offence against the Crown, the State and nature.

Storm

Storms, representing chaos in nature, are an apt image for the chaos caused by Duncan's murder. Storms are the Witches' element. The night of Duncan's murder is 'unruly'. Banquo's 'It will rain tonight' foreshadows the murder to come. The Apparitions are heralded by thunder and Ross says that fear causes Macbeth's subjects to 'float upon a wild and violent sea'.

Time

Time is stressed in the play's imagery, because it is linked to character and attitude. The guilt-free characters see time as a friendly or neutral presence. Macbeth initially feels that time is on his side, then that he can control it; finally it seems like an enemy to him, creeping on with death. With the return of Malcolm we are told that 'The time is free.'

Treachery

Treachery or treason are the opposite of loyalty, and signify the worst sin. The spirit of treachery pervades the play from the 'disloyal traitor' of the first Act, through Macbeth's breaking of Duncan's 'double trust', which Banquo calls 'treasonous malice'. Macbeth fears Banquo because he will keep 'allegiance clear'. In the end Macbeth suffers more from treachery than anybody else, since who can remain loyal to a traitor?

Water

Lady Macbeth sees water as all that is needed to cleanse them of murder. She is wrong, and Macbeth is right in his prophecy that even the ocean will not purify them. The healing powers of water and the pity of tears are not for the damned, and the recurrent water imagery underlines this.

Analysis chart

Act	Scene	Important events	Heathland/moor	Macbeth's castle: Inverness	Duncan's court:	Macduff's castle: Fife	London	Birnam Wood	Macbeth's castle: Dunsinane	Unspecified	Banquo	Duncan	Fleance	Lady Macbeth	Lady Macduff	Lennox	Macbeth
			Places								**Characters**						
1	1	The Witches set the tone of the play	●														
	2	Duncan decides to make Macbeth Thane of Cawdor			●						●	●		●			
	3	The Witches foretell the future for Banquo and Macbeth	●								●			●			
	4	Macbeth resolves to 'o'er leap' the problem of Malcolm			●						●	●					
	5	Lady Macbeth reads her husband's letter to her		●							●			●	●		
	6	Duncan arrives to stay at Macbeth's castle		●							●						
	7	Macbeth is persuaded by his wife to kill the King		●									●	●			
2	1	Macbeth sees the vision of the dagger		●							●		●				
	2	The murder of Duncan		●										●			
	3	The 'Porter Scene': Malcolm and Donalbain flee to safety		●							●			●		●	
	4	Macduff, Ross and an Old Man discuss events so far								●							
3	1	Macbeth arranges for the murder of Banquo and Fleance		●							●		●	●			
	2	Macbeth reassures his wife that all will soon be well		●									●	●			
	3	Banquo is murdered – Fleance escapes		●							●		●				
	4	The ghost of Banquo appears at Macbeth's banquet		●										●		●	
	5	The Witches say they will meet Macbeth again	●														●
	6	Echo of II.4, but with Lennox and another Lord								●						●	
4	1	The Apparitions' scene, set in a cave	●														●
	2	Macbeth has Macduff's wife and family murdered				●									●	●	
	3	Macduff vows to kill Macbeth					●										●
5	1	Lady Macbeth's 'sleepwalking' scene							●					●			
	2	The Scottish and English armies begin to gather against Macbeth								●						●	●
	3	Macbeth calls for his armour							●					●			●
	4	Branches from Birnam Wood are cut for camouflage						●									
	5	Lady Macbeth dies. Birnam Wood begins to 'move'							●								
	6	Macduff kills Macbeth in battle							●					●			

Themes

Macduff	Malcolm	Porter	Ross	Witches	Ambition	Animals	Aspects of style	Banquet	Blood	Chaos	Children	Clothing	Darkness	Dreams	Fate	Fear	Growth	Haste	Light	Loyalty	Noise	Order	Portents	Prophecy	Sickness	Sleep	Storm	The Crown	The State	Time	Treachery	Water	Page in commentary on which scene first appears
				•		•	•			•			•		•								•										19
	•		•	•		•	•		•						•			•	•			•	•							•	•	•	20
			•	•	•		•			•	•	•	•		•	•	•			•	•		•	•	•	•	•	•		•	•	•	22
	•				•			•					•				•		•	•										•	•		27
				•	•	•	•					•	•					•	•			•			•			•		•	•		29
				•	•	•			•						•															•			32
				•	•		•				•	•						•		•	•					•		•	•		•		32
				•			•		•				•	•								•			•					•			35
				•	•		•	•	•				•			•					•				•	•						•	36
•	•	•		•	•	•	•	•	•	•		•	•		•	•		•		•	•		•		•	•	•	•		•		•	38
			•		•	•	•			•			•	•		•		•	•		•	•			•		•			•			41
				•	•	•	•			•	•		•		•	•	•	•			•					•		•		•			43
						•				•	•			•		•				•		•			•						•		45
				•	•				•		•		•					•													•		46
			•			•		•	•	•	•		•		•	•	•	•			•				•	•						•	47
				•	•		•																										50
						•	•							•							•					•		•					50
				•		•	•			•	•		•		•	•	•						•		•	•	•			•	•		51
•			•		•					•	•				•	•				•						•				•	•		53
•	•		•			•	•		•		•	•			•		•			•	•	•		•	•					•	•		54
						•	•		•				•	•					•		•				•	•		•		•		•	58
			•			•	•		•		•	•			•					•					•	•				•			59
												•			•	•	•								•	•			•	•			60
				•																			•										61
						•	•					•			•			•		•				•		•					•		61
•	•		•		•	•									•	•				•	•	•				•					•		62

Finding your way around the commentary

Each page of the commentary gives the following information:

1 A quotation from the start of each paragraph on which a comment is made, or act/scene or line numbers plus a quotation, so that you can easily locate the right place in your text.

2 A series of comments, explaining, interpreting, and drawing your attention to important incidents, characters and aspects of the text.

3 For each comment, headings to indicate the important characters, themes, and ideas dealt with in the comment.

4 For each heading, a note of the comment numbers in this guide where the previous or next comment dealing with that heading occurred.

Thus you can use this commentary section in a number of ways.

1 Turn to that part of the commentary dealing with the chapter/act you are perhaps revising for a class discussion or essay. Read through the comments in sequence, referring all the time to the text, which you should have open before you. The comments will direct your attention to all the important things of which you should take note.

2 Take a single character or topic from the list on page 17. Note the comment number next to it. Turn to that comment in this guide, where you will find the first of a number of comments on your chosen topic. Study it, and the appropriate part of your text to which it will direct you. Note the comment number in this guide where the next comment for your topic occurs and turn to it when you are ready. Thus, you can follow one topic right through your text. If you have an essay to write on a particular character or theme just follow the path through this guide and you will soon find everything you need to know!

3 A number of relevant relationships between characters and topics are listed on page 18. To follow these relationships throughout your text, turn to the comment indicated. As the previous and next comment are printed at the side of each page in the commentary, it is a simple matter to flick through the pages to find the previous or next occurrence of the relationship in which you are interested.

For example, you want to examine in depth the theme of treachery in the play. Turning to the single topic list, you will find that this theme first occurs in comment 23. On turning to comment 23 you will discover a zero (0) in the place of the previous reference (because this is the first time that it has occurred) and the number 39 for the next reference. You now turn to comment 39 and find that the previous comment number is 23 (from where you have just been looking) and that the next reference is to comment 48, and so on throughout the text.

You also wish to trace the relationship between Macbeth and water throughout the play. From the relationships list, you are directed to comment 20. This is the first time that both Macbeth and water are discussed together and you will now discover that two different comment numbers are given for the subject under examination – numbers 21 and 32. This is because the imagery of water and the character of Macbeth are traced separately as well as together and you will have to continue tracing them separately until you finally come to comment 33 – the next occasion on which both Macbeth and water are discussed.

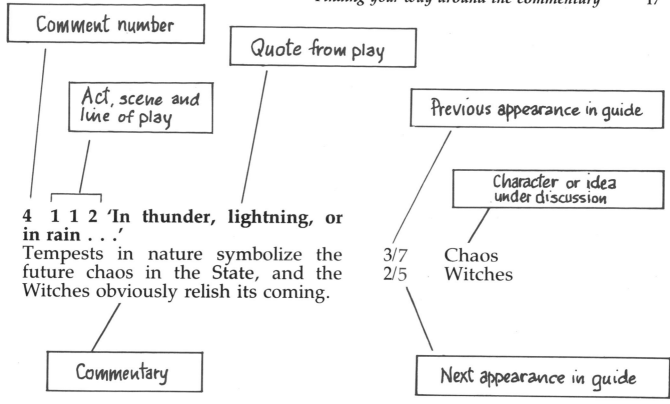

Comment number

Act, scene and line of play

Quote from play

Previous appearance in guide

Character or idea under discussion

4 1 1 2 'In thunder, lightning, or in rain . . .'
Tempests in nature symbolize the future chaos in the State, and the Witches obviously relish its coming.

3/7   Chaos
2/5   Witches

Commentary

Next appearance in guide

Single topics:

	Comment no:		Comment no:
Banquo	15	Ambition	30
Duncan	10	Animals	6
Fleance	132	Aspects of style	1
Lady Macbeth	24	Banquet	84
Lady Macduff	94	Blood	10
Lennox	181	Chaos	3
Macbeth	14	Children	59
Macduff	176	Clothing	57
Malcolm	11	Darkness	8
Porter	162	Dreams	135
Ross	22	Fate	5
Witches	1	Fear	46
		Growth	45
		Haste	22
		Light	79
		Loyalty	11
		Noise	37
		Order	14
		Portents	2
		Prophecy	47
		Sickness	51
		Sleep	34
		Storm	36
		The Crown	64
		The State	115
		Time	25
		Treachery	23
		Water	12

Relationships:

Almost any theme or image is likely to be found in interesting combinations with any of the major characters like Macbeth, Banquo, Lady Macbeth, for instance, but here are a few which you might perhaps not expect and which are revealing:

			Comment no:
Macbeth	and	Clothing	57
		Growth	45
		Haste	114
		Water	20
Lady Macbeth	and	Blood	160
		Darkness	149
		Sickness	150
		Water	160
Witches	and	Animals	6
		Treachery	48
Ambition	and	Chaos	61
		Order	81
Animals	and	Portents	95
Banquet	and	Chaos	168
		Order	84
Blood	and	Water	19
Children	and	Growth	214
Order	and	Ambition	81
		Banquet	84
Prophecy	and	Treachery	274
Time	and	Fate	69

Commentary

Act 1

1 1 1 1 'When shall we three . . .'
The Witches are the embodiment of evil. Their immediate introduction here indicates the theme of the play. Most of Shakespeare's audience would have believed in witches although their physical existence was beginning to be questioned by the society of the time. But the Witches have been depicted in *Macbeth* in such a way that they could just as easily be imaginary as real and both Banquo and Macbeth struggle with this paradox (i.e. apparent contradiction). The ambiguous nature of what is 'real' and the mixture of the rational and the superstitious produce a play which is timeless in the way it explores the nature of evil.

2 1 1 1 'When shall we three . . .'
The Witches are themselves the portents of evil things to come. They symbolize the forces of darkness–the darkness of night, of sickness, of death, of evil deeds and the spiritual and mental darkness of 'diseased' minds.

3 1 1 1 'When shall we three . . .'
Symbols of chaos open the action of the play, and never really leave the stage. We find constant echoes of the theme of chaos in the action (murders, betrayals, ambition) and in virtually every aspect of the imagery. In many ways the whole play is an affirmation of the powers of order and good eventually to overcome chaos and evil.

4 1 1 2 'In thunder, lightning, or in rain?'
Tempests in nature symbolize the future chaos in the State, and the Witches obviously relish its coming.

5 1 1 7 'There to meet with Macbeth.'
The Witches are agents of fate, but why might fate want to destroy Macbeth? Does there have to be a reason for the play to be effective, or does the reason not matter?

6 1 1 8 'I come, Grey-Malkin.'
Evil is often suggested by animal imagery in the play. Grey-Malkin and Padock are supernatural spirits in animal form ('familiars') which advise the Witches.

7 1 1 9 'Fair is foul, and foul is fair.'
To the Witches good (fair), is evil (foul), and evil is a good thing. Inspired by the Witches, Macbeth's tyranny will produce just the sort of chaos they talk about here.

8 1 1 10 'Hover through the fog . . .'
Darkness is the Witches' natural element. Most people instinctively avoid it, but Macbeth and Lady Macbeth will be dragged into it. Study Lady Macbeth's 'Hell is murky' speech in the sleepwalking scene.

	Characters and ideas previous/next comment
0/9	Aspects of style
0/2	Witches
0/16	Portents
1/4	Witches
0/4	Chaos
3/7	Chaos
2/5	Witches
0/13	Fate
4/6	Witches
0/17	Animals
5/7	Witches
4/31	Chaos
6/8	Witches
0/30	Darkness
7/26	Witches

9   1 2 1 'What bloody man is that?'
This scene forms a contrast with the previous one. There are no moral complications here, only basic issues of loyalty and treason, bravery and cowardice.

1/16	Aspects of style

10   1 2 1 'What bloody man is that?'
Why is it dramatically ironic that it is the King who first introduces the theme of bleeding and blood? Immediately after the Witches have opened the play, the first reference is to blood. Imagery related to blood appears throughout the play, often in subtle association with that of water. Macbeth's great blood-bath is seen not just as literally horrific – after all his grisly battlefield actions are applauded at the start of the play – but as symbolic. Civilization (or order) is being bled to death by the forces of chaos.

0/19	Blood
0/25	Duncan

11   1 2 3 'This is the sergeant . . .'
Compare this incident with the meeting between Macduff and Malcolm after Lady Macduff's murder. Malcolm is a character who values loyalty. The captain uses very inflated 'flowery' language and this is deliberate – in Shakespeare's day it would be felt appropriate that his kind of speech be used for passionate or weighty matters, and you will find other uses of such language – just before Banquo and Duncan go into Macbeth's castle, for example. The word 'captain' is replaced by 'sergeant' in some editions of the play, but you should not confuse either of these with the modern military equivalents.

0/21	Loyalty
0/70	Malcolm

12   1 2 8 'As two spent swimmers that do . . .'
Water is a complex image in the play. Even today, for what kinds of thing do we often use water as a symbol?

0/19	Water

13   1 2 14 'And fortune on his damnèd quarrel . . .'
Notice how fate (or fortune) is always accepted as unpredictable, except by Macbeth. Here his 'disdaining' is regarded as admirable. Think carefully – why is this same quality in him not also admired later in the play?

5/27	Fate

14   1 2 16 'For brave Macbeth . . .'
Macbeth's savagery is used here as an instrument of order. If the State regards this as admirable, why is the same behaviour not also admired later on, in a different context? Is the State acting in a hypocritical manner? If so, would it be right to think that this is something peculiar only to Macbeth's time?

0/15	Macbeth
0/18	Order

15   1 2 16 'For brave Macbeth . . .'
At the start of the play Macbeth and Banquo are comrades-in-arms, and are both depicted as terrifying warriors. However we see Macbeth singled out for mention by the Captain and for reward by the King.

0/20	Banquo
14/17	Macbeth

16   1 2 26 'Shipwracking storms and direful thunders;'
Water and storm imagery may be seen in these lines as portents of the future.

Line 31 mentions 'the Norweyan lord', although the sources say 'Danish'. It is thought that this is because *Macbeth* was first performed before the king

2/41	Portents
9/29	Aspects of style

(James I) and his brother-in-law King Christian IV of Denmark, on the latter's visit to England between July and August 1606. We know that Shakespeare's Company was performing before King James at Hampton Court on 7 August 1606, and this seems the most likely occasion for *Macbeth* to be staged. The change from Danish to Norwegian is therefore thought to be an amendment made to avoid giving offense.

17   1 2 35 'As sparrows, eagles, or the hare, . . .'
The Captain compares Macbeth and Banquo to eagles and lions. As the play progresses, notice how Macbeth is identified with animals lower and lower down the ladder of creation, until near the end of the play he is referred to as a 'weed' (by Lennox) and a 'monster' (by Macduff).

6/18	Animals
15/20	Macbeth

18   1 2 35 'As sparrows, eagles, or the hare, . . .'
Eagles and lions are admired for their power and beauty in the natural order of things. Macbeth will become another terrifying predator when he upsets this order.

17/95	Animals
14/25	Order

19   1 2 40 'Except they meant to bathe . . .'
This is a portent of future events. Notice the way the actions of bathing (usually associated with water) and blood are used in the imagery.

10/20	Blood
12/20	Water

20   1 2 40 'Except they meant to bathe . . .'
Notice the dramatic irony – later in the play Banquo will indeed 'bathe' in reeking wounds, as will Macbeth (in a slightly different sense). But who is really responsible for inflicting these wounds? Perhaps it is Macbeth but it may be Banquo, the Witches, or even Fate.

15/28	Banquo
19/142	Blood
17/21	Macbeth
19/32	Water

For Macbeth's own vision of bathing in reeking wounds, look at his 'I am in blood stepped in so far . . .' speech in Act 3.

Images of water and bathing abound in the play. Often water is seen as mighty and uncontrollable (the sea), sometimes it represents purity (holy water), and sometimes it appears close to images of blood, as here.

Golgotha was another name for Calvary, or the Place of The Skull. The original Hebrew 'gulgoleth' meant skull.

21   1 2 44 'So well thy words become thee . . .'
Duncan and Malcolm value loyalty. In this scene, we see Macbeth as a loyal subject. What makes him forget this loyalty?

11/54	Loyalty
20/24	Macbeth

22   1 2 46 'What a haste looks through his eyes!'
Here is an image of hurrying. Shakespeare uses messengers to move the action of the play along. Notice how often Ross is used to impart news either to the other characters or the audience. Here for example it seems that he was present at both battles, judging by the news he bears and his knowledge of the decisions which Macbeth had made.

0/106	Haste
0/54	Ross

23   1 2 54 'Assisted by that most disloyal traitor, . . .'
The first reference to treachery is linked with the name of Cawdor. Why is this ironic?

0/39	Treachery

	Characters and ideas previous/next comment

24   1 2 56 'Till that Bellona's bridegroom, . . .'
'Bellona's bridegroom': consider the significance of this description of Macbeth as the husband of the goddess of war, rather than as the actual god of war himself.

0/34	Lady Macbeth
21/26	Macbeth

25   1 2 66 'No more that Thane of Cawdor . . .'
Duncan has a well-developed sense of justice and order, and acts quickly here. Why does he not see the developing threat from Macbeth? This is an introduction to the theme of time in the play. Duncan is talking only of the past, but Macbeth will try to control the future.

In medieval Scotland a Thane was a person of rank, often the chief of a Clan, who held land given to him by the King.

10/72	Duncan
18/74	Order
0/44	Time

26   1 2 70 'What he hath lost, . . .'
Compare this with the first few lines of the play. Listen for other such echoes as you study the play, as they reveal subtle links between the action and the characterization.

24/27	Macbeth
8/29	Witches

27   1 2 70 'What he hath lost, . . .'
This is an apparent stroke of good fortune for Macbeth. Was it fate that made this the beginning of his misfortunes too? Notice how Macbeth is depicted in his absence as a brave and strong soldier, a brilliant general and a man accustomed to assuming authority. Notice how these characteristics change as the play progresses. Does he retain any of these qualities at the end of the play?

13/38	Fate
26/28	Macbeth

28   1 3 1 'Where hast thou been, sister?'
Notice in this scene how Macbeth and Banquo differ in their reaction to the Witches. At line 50 is Banquo (the innocent) looking at Macbeth (the guilty) in a new light?

20/42	Banquo
27/33	Macbeth

29   1 3 1 'Where hast thou been, sister?'
In this scene, the themes of the previous two scenes mingle as the valiant Thanes meet the forces of evil.

16/63	Aspects of style
26/31	Witches

30   1 3 1 'Where hast thou been, sister?'
The scene direction here specifies thunder and we may therefore imagine that this meeting takes place in gloom, if not in darkness. This grey and gloomy world is the one which opens the play. It is in this darkness of night and of the mind that Macbeth's spark of ambition is fuelled.

0/43	Ambition
8/62	Darkness

31   1 3 4 'A sailor's wife had chestnuts . . .'
We already know the Witches are evil; now we are given some idea of their power.

Witchcraft was punishable by death in English law, by an Act of 1604; King James was an authority on it and had published his book 'Demonologie' on the subject. The topicality of the play for Hampton Court in August 1606 (see paragraph 16) must have been enhanced by the fact that King James had been subject to the practice of witchcraft already. After marrying King Christian's sister Anne, James returned from Denmark to England by sea and found his passage delayed by difficult winds. A coven of witches was

7/35	Chaos
29/35	Witches

caught and confessed that they had tried to poison the King with a toad's venom; when that did not work they had christened a cat, tied bits of a dead man to it (look at paragraph 263) and then 'sailing in their riddles or sieves' had left it off the port of Leith, which had caused the storm which delayed the King. This is alluded to around line 8 here.

---

32   1 3 4 'A sailor's wife had chestnuts . . .'
The time of Shakespeare was one of great voyages. The sea represented the unknown and uncontrollable forces of nature, promising great fortunes, discoveries and adventures, but also threatening chaos and destruction. So to the Elizabethan mind the spirit of evil could be associated with water, as it is here.

20/33   Water

---

33   1 3 18 'I'll drain him dry as hay;'
The sailor's ship, at the mercy of the sea, is a metaphor for the ship of State with Macbeth as captain. Although it 'cannot be lost' (sunk), 'yet it shall be tempest-tossed'.

28/34   Macbeth
32/155   Water

---

34   1 3 19 'Sleep shall neither night nor day . . .'
This is the first reference to sleep. Macbeth and Lady Macbeth will undergo the same torture. The Witches will deprive the sailor of sleep as a punishment for his wife's 'wickedness' (as the first Witch sees it). Lady Macbeth will be similarly tortured. Why?

Notice how, at different times during the play, sleep is depicted as the 'counterfeit' of life and the dead as being 'but pictures'. How true is this view of sleep with reference to Banquo, Duncan and Macbeth?

24/88   Lady Macbeth
33/36   Macbeth
0/122   Sleep

---

35   1 3 24 'Though his bark cannot be lost, . . .'
Examine this passage and note how the power of the Witches is limited; they can create the climate for evil but only man can actually cause the ultimate chaos, the destruction of order in the world. They cannot sink this ship, but Macbeth will sink his 'ship' (the State), through his own actions.

31/61   Chaos
31/38   Witches

---

36   1 3 24 'Though his bark cannot be lost, . . .'
The Witches will torment the sailor with terrible storms. Macbeth enters to the beating of a drum. Images of storm and noise surround Macbeth throughout the play. He is at the centre of the play's storms.

34/39   Macbeth
0/171   Storm

---

37   1 3 29 'A drum! a drum!'
This is Macbeth's first appearance. Is he always to be associated with 'sound and . . .' and if you can complete the quote, what does this tell you about Macbeth's struggle for power?

0/130   Noise

---

38   1 3 31 'The Weird Sisters, hand in hand, . . .'
The 'Weird Sisters' (the Witches), acting as the three Fates or Destinies, seek to influence the fate of Macbeth. ('Wyrd' was the Anglo-Saxon word for fate.)

27/58   Fate
35/40   Witches

---

39 1 3 36 'Peace! The charm's wound up.'
The Witches concoct a 'charm' to work upon Macbeth, whose treachery is in many senses not 'natural'.

36/40	Macbeth
23/48	Treachery

---

40 1 3 37 'So foul and fair a day . . .'
Macbeth is merely contrasting the foul weather and the splendid events of the day. What is interesting about the words he chooses, and what is their dramatic effect?

39/43	Macbeth
38/42	Witches

---

41 1 3 37 'So foul and fair a day . . .'
The play is full of portents. Characters like the Witches are themselves portents. References to animals and events are interwoven with the play's imagery to heighten the sense of atmosphere and the symbolism. For example, at the start of the play, notice how Macbeth's first words echo those of the Witches; he seems to have stepped into their world.

16/95	Portents

---

42 1 3 38 'How far is't called to Forres?'
Consider Banquo's reasons for his suspicion that the Witches are not what they seem. What does this tell you about them? Banquo, not Macbeth, is the one who so vividly describes the Witches. Does this strike you as subtly appropriate? Does he see them more clearly than his partner, in more ways than one?

28/45	Banquo
40/47	Witches

---

43 1 3 50 'Good sir, why do you start, . . .'
Have the Witches in their prophecy spoken Macbeth's secret ambition?

30/49	Ambition
40/45	Macbeth

---

44 1 3 57 'If you can look into the seeds of time . . .'
To Banquo, the idea of looking into 'the seeds of time' is fantastic. Macbeth is immediately attracted by the idea.

25/69	Time

---

45 1 3 57 'If you can look into the seeds of time . . .'
What 'seeds' of Banquo's will grow in the future? Growth, when associated with Banquo, is of a natural kind – what about Macbeth? Think about the 'seeds' that have been planted by the Witches. Whose 'seeds' will Macbeth come to fear? Notice how images of natural things, like growth, are used to counterpoint Macbeth's 'growth'.

42/46	Banquo
0/76	Growth
43/49	Macbeth

---

46 1 3 59 'Speak then to me who . . .'
Why has Banquo nothing to fear? Think about what Macbeth does have to fear.

45/52	Banquo
0/55	Fear

---

47 1 3 64 'Lesser than Macbeth, and greater.'
The Witches often hide truth in the ambiguous way in which they say things. Why is Macbeth's reaction to this prophecy different from that of Banquo? Most of the play's prophecies are uttered by the Witches, but some are spoken by Macbeth and Banquo – often unconsciously it seems. Prophecies are usually deliberately vague, so as to intrigue us and heighten dramatic tension. This is typical of the Witches – their prophecies are hidden in such impenetrable riddles that what they mean is what Macbeth and Banquo want them to mean.

0/60	Prophecy
42/48	Witches

Characters and ideas previous/next comment

	Characters and ideas *previous/next comment*

48 1 3 69 'Stay, you imperfect speakers!'
The Witches intended from the start that Macbeth should be the target for their evil. They are treacherous because they say things in ways that lead men to draw the wrong conclusions. The Witches play upon Macbeth's weakness to betray him, just as Macbeth preys on those of Duncan. (What weaknesses has Duncan? Think about how many people betray him. Was he an unfit King?)

39/72	Treachery
47/49	Witches

49 1 3 71 'But how of Cawdor?'
What does Macbeth's reaction tell us about his state of mind? Read this speech carefully; does Macbeth actually want to believe the Witches? Look at his letter to his wife and consider whether it is his over-eagerness to be convinced which dooms him.

43/50	Ambition
54/50	Macbeth
48/60	Witches

50 1 3 80 'Into the air; and what seemed corporal . . .'
Macbeth is not only speaking of the Witches. What else has just disappeared from his life? (Hint: look at his speech in Act 5, scene 3, around line 20.)

49/52	Ambition
49/51	Macbeth

51 1 3 83 'Or have we eaten on the insane root . . .'
Is this ironic? What 'sickness' does Macbeth suffer from?

50/53	Macbeth
0/91	Sickness

52 1 3 83 'Or have we eaten on the insane root . . .'
The Witches seem unable to mesmerize Banquo in the way they have Macbeth. He is probably able to be so sceptical of them because he has no hidden ambitions.

50/59	Ambition
46/56	Banquo

53 1 3 85 'Your children shall be kings.'
Fear becomes associated with children in Macbeth's mind. Why?

0/59	Children
51/55	Macbeth

54 1 3 88 'The King hath happily received . . .'
The trustworthy Ross is the messenger again. He is loyal both to Duncan and, when he is King, to Macbeth. Compare his admiration for Macbeth now to his opinion in Act 4.

21/70	Loyalty
22/190	Ross

55 1 3 95 'Nothing afeard of what thyself . . .'
Macbeth has no fear of the distorted bodies he leaves on the battlefield. Compare this with his reaction to Duncan's body immediately after the murder.

46/157	Fear
53/57	Macbeth

56 1 3 106 'What! Can the devil speak true?'
How convinced is Banquo? What does his choice of words show us?

52/60	Banquo

57 1 3 107 'The Thane of Cawdor lives.'
The image of borrowed robes recurs in the play, representing the taking of somebody else's place. What other attribute of Cawdor's may Macbeth also have assumed?

0/69	Clothing
55/58	Macbeth

58   1 3 114 'But treasons capital, confessed, . . .'
Macbeth is blind to this warning by fate.

38/67   Fate
57/59   Macbeth

---

59   1 3 117 'Do you not hope your children . . .'
Macbeth already sees Banquo's children as a threat to his future greatness.
This is the second time that Macbeth has mentioned that Banquo's children
may be kings. Why is he so concerned about this? Is he not satisfied that the
Witches say he is to be king? Or is he just overwhelmingly happy for his
friend?

52/61   Ambition
53/78   Children
58/63   Macbeth

---

60   1 3 121 'Besides the Thane of Cawdor.'
Banquo senses that the Witches are a force for evil, but he knows that men
cannot be forced into evil against their own will. Actions only become really
evil when they are driven by evil intentions. Contrast this with Macbeth's
reaction. Notice that he already talks of murder. The Witches are not the
only characters in the play who make prophecies. Why is Macbeth so
receptive to the prophecies made by the spirits of darkness, yet deaf to this
one from his friend? Unlike Macbeth, Banquo realizes that evil spirits and
prophecies are not to be trusted. Note that anything else is a 'trifle'
compared to the Crown.

56/77   Banquo
47/269   Prophecy
49/62   Witches

---

61   1 3 122 'And oftentimes, to win us to our harm, . . .'
Banquo sees here that the Witches' words are temptations which lead into
the world of darkness and chaos.

59/64   Ambition
35/65   Chaos

---

62   1 3 123 'The instruments of darkness . . .'
Banquo is in no doubt that the 'instruments of darkness' represent evil.
Compare this with Macbeth's attitude below. Why do you think they react
so differently?

30/83   Darkness
60/92   Witches

---

63   1 3 126 'Two truths are told . . .'
This is more of a prolonged aside than a soliloquy, but this speech confirms
our suspicion that Macbeth is tempted by the Witches' prophecies. He is,
literally, talking himself into the idea that Duncan's murder is a possibility, if
a frightening one.

29/85   Aspects
         of style
59/65   Macbeth

---

64   1 3 127 'As happy prologues to the swelling Act . . .'
This 'aside' of Macbeth's shows his dilemma clearly; the 'imperial theme'
(his rise to kingship) is 'swelling' (becoming louder and more strident). Was
Macbeth a man who was tempted too far? Is it true of all people, that they
have secret desires which they will do almost anything to realize?

61/66   Ambition
0/102   The Crown

---

65   1 3 129 'This supernatural soliciting . . .'
There is chaos in the mind of Macbeth as he attempts to compromise with
evil.

61/168   Chaos
63/66   Macbeth

---

66   1 3 133 'If good, why do I yield . . .'
What is the 'suggestion' that Macbeth fears? Who is doing the 'suggesting'?

64/75   Ambition
65/67   Macbeth

	Characters and ideas previous/next comment

67 1 3 138 'My thought, whose murder yet is . . .'
Macbeth is being overwhelmed by events and 'now will his bark be tempest tossed'. Does his destiny lie within his own control? Does Macbeth believe that it is?

| 58/69 | Fate |
| 66/68 | Macbeth |

68 1 3 145 'Like our strange garments, . . .'
It takes time to feel comfortable in new clothes, suggests Banquo. Consider the effect that the 'borrowed robes' have on Macbeth.

| 57/87 | Clothing |
| 67/71 | Macbeth |

69 1 3 147 'Time and the hour runs through . . .'
Macbeth regards time as a force like fate—something beyond his power to control. Later, he will think he can manipulate it.

| 67/178 | Fate |
| 44/73 | Time |

70 1 4 8 'A deep repentance.'
In Malcolm's mind the Thane of Cawdor's soul is saved by his ultimate loyalty and repentance. Compare this with Macbeth's state of mind before his death.

| 54/71 | Loyalty |
| 11/186 | Malcolm |

71 1 4 11 'To throw away the dearest thing . . .'
Is Macbeth about to 'throw away' everything of value in his life, and what exactly might this be?

| 70/185 | Loyalty |
| 68/73 | Macbeth |

72 1 4 12 'There's no art . . .'
Here is great dramatic irony. To whom else could this speech refer?

| 25/74 | Duncan |
| 48/82 | Treachery |

73 1 4 18 'That swiftest wing of recompense . . .'
Note the irony. Macbeth will indeed be recompensed in the end, in many ways!

| 71/75 | Macbeth |
| 69/100 | Time |

74 1 4 22 ' "More is thy due than more . . ." '
Does Macbeth really deserve such extreme rewards? Duncan seems to be encouraging in Macbeth the sin (to the Elizabethans) of wanting to raise himself above his natural station in the order of things. It would be true to say that Duncan's fate is at least partly his own fault.

| 72/76 | Duncan |
| 25/81 | Order |

75 1 4 22 ' "More is thy due than more . . ." '
The King (unwittingly) tempts Macbeth's ambition with his praise. Macbeth will arrange to 'pay' himself.

| 66/77 | Ambition |
| 73/80 | Macbeth |

76 1 4 29 'I have begun to plant thee, . . .'
Here are ironic images of growth, but who has sown the seeds and what is it that is growing in Macbeth? Duncan introduces the imagery of growth, and the way he uses it allows us to see that it is a contrasting theme in the play to ambition. Advancement by the king (God's agent) is natural and proper, and therefore opposed to ambition, which is a desire to advance oneself beyond one's current status or place. We might find this notion rather curious, but it had a central and important place in the society of Shakespeare's time.

| 74/78 | Duncan |
| 45/203 | Growth |

	Characters and ideas	
	previous/next comment	

77   1 4 33 'There if I grow, . . .'
Does Banquo's reply to the King show that he is happy just to serve the monarch? Later on he is just as loyal to Macbeth as king, even though he suspects foul play. Banquo might have behaved differently if he had ambition.

75/80 Ambition
60/86 Banquo

---

78   1 4 39 'Our eldest, Malcolm, . . .'
Here Duncan continues the idea, first seen in the speech of the Witches, that children are the key to the future. Duncan announces that his son Malcolm will succeed him on the throne.

59/118 Children
76/84 Duncan

---

79   1 4 42 'But signs of nobleness, like stars, . . .'
The Heavens, stars and light are here associated with honour, as Macbeth acknowledges in his next aside.

0/83 Light

---

80   1 4 49 'The Prince of Cumberland! That is a step . . .'
Macbeth realizes that he must act if he is to turn fate to serve his ambition.

Is Macbeth already planning beyond the death of Duncan before we even meet Lady Macbeth, or is it she who first thinks of murdering the King?

77/81 Ambition
75/82 Macbeth

---

81   1 4 49 'The Prince of Cumberland! That is a step . . .'
Every person and thing had a particular place in the natural (ordered) scheme of things. Ambition was seen as dangerous to this, because it caused people to want to elevate themselves above their 'natural state.'

80/88 Ambition
74/84 Order

---

82   1 4 51 'For in my way it lies.'
Darkness is growing in Macbeth's mind; he feels the need to hide from the light, which is symbolic of heaven.

80/86 Macbeth
72/101 Treachery

---

83   1 4 51 'For in my way it lies.'
The imagery of darkness and light is common in Shakespeare, and strikes much the same moral and religious echoes now as it would have done in his time.

62/98 Darkness
79/99 Light

---

84   1 4 57 'It is a banquet to me.'
Duncan introduces the banqueting imagery in the play, and establishes it as a wholesome analogy for orderliness and proper conduct.

0/152 Banquet
78/116 Duncan
81/115 Order

Think about the use of this imagery following the banquet given for Duncan, and in the banquet scene after Macbeth has become king. Images of eating, drinking, food and banqueting run throughout the play. Macbeth is a 'banquet' to Duncan; Macbeth describes sleep as 'the chief nourisher in life's feast' (Act 2, scene 2); the Porter outlines the dangers of too much indulgence in a good thing (Act 2, scene 3). Eventually however, the 'great feast' which Lady Macbeth desired is unpalatable, and Macbeth finds he has 'supped full with horrors', which is an interesting inversion of the imagery's use so far (look at comment 347). There have been references to food and eating already in the play (by the Witches and Banquo), but Duncan introduces the imagery of banqueting proper. Feasting in the play is usually a symbol for the forces of life and order, which is why the Lord's comment to Lennox, 'Free from our feasts and banquets bloody knives' is appropriate (look at comment 260). This imagery is often connected with Macbeth and Lady Macbeth.

85 1 5 1 *'They met me in the day of success, . . .'*
At more than one point in the play a character, or in this interesting case, a letter, gives a summary of the action so far (a sort of narrator, or 'Chorus'). Here the device also gives us more information about Macbeth by using a clever form of soliloquy.

The use of language in the play is especially rich. We have already seen the 'courtly' speech of Macbeth and Lady Macbeth (receiving honours from Duncan; welcoming him to their castle), and the 'flowery' and ornate reporting of the Captain. We shall soon see the broken verse of the Macbeths after the murder, which is similar to Macduff's verse after he is told about the murder of his family. Comparing these last two is interesting – see how the first is nervous, twitchy and tense, whilst Macduff's is at first flat and even.

Notice also the down-to-earth wit of the Porter, the affectionate teasing of Lady Macduff and her son, and Lady Macbeth's 'broken' verse in her sleepwalking.

There is also more rhyme in *Macbeth* than we might expect in such a serious play. Much of this originates with the Witches of course, whose incantations suit rhyme, but there are also many occasional rhymed couplets in the play which are used to accentuate important points. Rhymed couplets are also found in their more usual guise as a device to 'close' scenes.

63/89	Aspects of style

86 1 5 3 *'. . . When I burned in desire to question . . .'*
The letter reveals how eagerly Macbeth embraced the temptation offered by the Witches. Contrast this with Banquo's reaction and try to decide why there is such a difference.

77/110	Banquo
82/105	Macbeth

87 1 5 5 *'Whiles I stood rapt in the wonder . . .'*
This is not the first reference to 'rapt'. Find the others and note how they echo and emphasize the theme of clothing. See how in this instance the pun also connects the theme of clothing to those of dreams and sleep. Plays on the sounds and meanings of words are common in Shakespeare's works.

68/98	Clothing

88 1 5 11 *'. . . rejoicing by being ignorant of what greatness, . . .'*
Macbeth emphasizes that Lady Macbeth will share his greatness. Is this possibility particularly important to her, do you think?

81/90	Ambition
34/89	Lady Macbeth

89 1 5 13 **'Glamis thou art, and Cawdor . . .'**
This soliloquy quickly impresses on us two important facts about Lady Macbeth – her determination and her knowledge of her husband's character.

85/93	Aspects of style
88/90	Lady Macbeth

90 1 5 14 **'What thou art promised.'**
Lady Macbeth has obviously thought about acquiring power and has considered her husband's lack of the necessary drive – which she possesses.

88/91	Ambition
88/92	Lady Macbeth

91 1 5 18 **'The illness should attend it.'**
The 'illness' which Lady Macbeth refers to here is wickedness. A certain amount of ambition is normal in people, provided it is not fuelled and fanned to excess.

90/97	Ambition
51/150	Sickness

92   1 5 23 'Than wishest should be undone.'
'Woman will lead man to destruction'. This ancient theme in literature was often used by Shakespeare. What have Lady Macbeth and the Witches in common?

90/93	Lady Macbeth
62/96	Witches

93   1 5 36 'He brings great news.'
A soliloquy tells us things about a character, which that character would not confess 'in public'. In this case we learn of Lady Macbeth's obsessive streak, which overcomes imagination, conscience and even common sense. What she does not realize until much later in the play is that by trying to wipe out Macbeth's sense of pity and duty she is actually seeking to destroy all that is human in him. This whole soliloquy of hers is an acceptance of the inverted values of the Witches.

89/109	Aspects of style
92/94	Lady Macbeth

94   1 5 36 'The raven himself . . .'
Compare this first appearance of Lady Macbeth with the single appearance of Lady Macduff. Lady Macduff, unlike Lady Macbeth, appears in playful and loving association with the innocent wisdom of childhood. Lady Macbeth and her husband have rather different attitudes towards children.

93/96	Lady Macbeth
0/281	Lady Macduff

95   1 5 36 'The raven himself . . .'
The raven, representing death, is foreshadowing the events to come.

18/105	Animals
41/140	Portents

96   1 5 38 'Under my battlements.'
Lady Macbeth's incantation echoes the chanting rhythms of the Witches, although its prose (as opposed to the Witches' rhyming couplets) considerably heightens the dramatic tension.

94/97	Lady Macbeth
92/104	Witches

97   1 5 41 'Of direst cruelty. Make thick my blood;'
Lady Macbeth knows that human feelings must be obliterated in the single-minded fight for power.

91/101	Ambition
96/98	Lady Macbeth

98   1 5 48 'You wait on nature's mischief.'
Evil flourishes best in darkness, hidden from the gaze of Heaven. The 'smoke of Hell' suggests the same atmosphere as the Witches' 'fog and filthy air'. Lady Macbeth talks a lot about hiding their intentions. She wants Macbeth to be like a snake hiding under a flower – to put on a false face. Here she calls for the 'blanket of the dark' to conceal their deeds. The imagery of clothing is always associated with Lord and Lady Macbeth. These images continue the idea of outside appearance (clothing) as a 'false face', hence the wish of Lady Macbeth that her deeds be concealed or 'blanketed' from Heaven.

87/121	Clothing
83/133	Darkness
97/100	Lady Macbeth

99   1 5 48 'You wait on nature's mischief.'
The King is the divine symbol of God on earth, and is accordingly talked about metaphorically as the sun, the stars and light in general. The Macbeths' descent into darkness is therefore heavy with symbolism. Evil deeds must be hidden from the stars. Night and day become confused in the real world, and in the mind of Lady Macbeth, after Duncan's murder.

83/191	Light

100 1 5 55 'This ignorant present, . . .'
Lady Macbeth already begins to feel that she and her husband can control time and make the future do what they want.

| 98/103 | Lady Macbeth |
| 73/112 | Time |

101 1 5 58 'O never/Shall sun . . .'
Lady Macbeth's ambition manifests itself almost at once as treacherous plotting against Duncan, who is Macbeth's greatest benefactor.

| 97/108 | Ambition |
| 82/103 | Treachery |

102 1 5 59 'Shall sun that morrow see!'
Sun and light are symbolic of the Crown, representing order and goodness. All of these are about to be eclipsed.

| 64/116 | The Crown |

103 1 5 60 'Your face, my thane, is as a book . . .'
Lady Macbeth has already decided on the murder. Her only worry is that Macbeth will give himself away. Compare her observation with Duncan's earlier remark about the previous Thane of Cawdor.

| 100/104 | Lady Macbeth |
| 101/122 | Treachery |

104 1 5 60 'Your face, my thane, is as a book . . .'
What did the Witches read in Macbeth's face? Notice how easily Lady Macbeth has assumed the role of leader in the murder. Could she be compared to a witch?

Which other prophecies come true by Macbeth's own actions and which by the actions of others?

| 103/106 | Lady Macbeth |
| 96/127 | Witches |

105 1 5 64 'But be the serpent under't . . .'
Macbeth is tempted by his wife to become a 'serpent'. This is an interesting reversal of a biblical image from Genesis.

A plot to kill the King was a very topical subject of the day, and this comment of Lady Macbeth's might also be a reference to the medal struck to commemorate the famous Gunpowder Plot of November 1605. The medal shows a serpent concealed underneath flowers.

It has also been suggested that one of the Gunpowder Plot's conspirators, a man called Sir Everard Digby, is referred to in Duncan's 'He was a gentleman on whom I built an absolute trust'. Digby was a particular favourite of the King.

| 95/111 | Animals |
| 86/107 | Macbeth |

106 1 5 66 'This night's great business . . .'
Lady Macbeth remains convinced that a single act will secure their future. Her lack of imagination contributes to their downfall.

| 22/113 | Haste |
| 104/107 | Lady Macbeth |

107 1 5 66 'This night's great business . . .'
Compare this with Macbeth's soliloquy at the start of Act 1, scene 7, to appreciate the difference in their characters.

| 106/108 | Lady Macbeth |
| 105/110 | Macbeth |

108 1 5 66 'This night's great business . . .'
So far Lady Macbeth has shown determination to assist her husband to power. Here she identifies herself with future glory.

| 101/119 | Ambition |
| 107/123 | Lady Macbeth |

109   1 6 1 'This castle hath a pleasant seat . . .'
We have here a peaceful, lyrical interlude before being plunged into more evil. Note the dramatic contrast between the relaxed atmosphere outside the castle and the tension within it. The castle seems to be following Lady Macbeth's advice to her husband! (Look at comments 95 and 105.)

93/114	Aspects of style

110   1 6 3 'This guest of summer, . . .'
It is interesting that it should be Banquo who talks about the beautiful surroundings of Macbeth's castle. In the previous scene we saw the Macbeths planning to put a false face on their intentions, and in the Porter scene we see the castle entrance depicted as the gateway to Hell.

86/134	Banquo
107/112	Macbeth

111   1 6 4 'The temple-haunting martlet, . . .'
Compare the gentle Banquo's observation of the sweet air loved by the martlet, with Lady Macbeth's image of the croaking raven in the last scene.

105/145	Animals

112   1 6 20 'Where's the Thane of Cawdor?'
This is a re-emphasis of the sense of urgency associated with Macbeth, the speed with which events are moving, and the way in which he is now trying to overtake and control time. Interestingly, Macbeth is not present at this formal welcome.

110/114	Macbeth
100/169	Time

113   1 6 21 'We coursed him at the heels . . .'
A central theme of the play is the importance of the natural order and sequence of things. In seeking to bend events to his will, Macbeth tries to outrun nature's normal pace. Everywhere Macbeth goes he seems to hurry at breakneck speed, as though he feels he will succeed if only he can go fast enough. At the start of the play he rushes to his castle to greet the King, and at the end he curses Seyton in his impatience to don his armour before it is time. Between these two events he comes to realize that time's 'petty pace' cannot be usurped, and he is left stranded (as he feared in Act 1, scene 7) on his 'bank and shoal of time'.

106/114	Haste

114   1 7 1 'If it were done when 'tis done, . . .'
This is a good example of dramatic tension. Will they or won't they murder Duncan? The audience is kept in suspense. We are allowed to realize that Macbeth has a conscience and some imagination, unlike Lady Macbeth. His better self realizes that to murder the King would be morally and politically wrong, so we know we are not dealing with the totally black-hearted villain of melodrama. Macbeth is a man of action, but the rightness or otherwise of his proposed action is something of a mental minefield for him. Compare this with his decisiveness in battle.

109/132	Aspects of style
113/187	Haste
112/115	Macbeth

Macbeth's imagery is very revealing: it seems to suggest that this world is temporary and impermanent, a 'bank and shoal of time' which will be washed away in the sea of eternity; it is the eternal spiritual values like honour and loyalty which matter, not earthly success and riches. This contrast between what he says and what his words imply is a highly effective way of showing his own inner turmoil about what he should do. His deeper insight proves in the end to have been true.

115   1 7 12 'To our own lips. He's here . . .'
Macbeth explains to himself (and to us) why he should not murder Duncan. To what extent is he convinced by his own argument? You will find that a

114/118	Macbeth
84/117	Order

clear understanding of this speech will help you a great deal in your study of the play. Macbeth explains to the audience that he sees the implications in doing what he is considering, implications for the state and for natural order. Duncan's virtues are so many and so good that they, 'like angels', would cry out at his murder.

This speech neatly catches the spirit of the age; an age steeped in traditional medieval beliefs about 'damnation' and 'sacrilegeous murder', and yet an age which was starting to question its own ideas about the nature of Kingship, the nature of God, the validity of superstition and so on. *Macbeth* has been described as a play which affirms the triumph of good over evil, but it is a triumph which is not achieved without doubt and struggle.

	0/293	The State

116   1 7 16 'Not bear the knife myself.'
Macbeth is aware of the noble qualities of Duncan the King. Contrast this with Macbeth's own reign later in the play.

84/120	Duncan
102/186	The Crown

117   1 7 21 'And Pity, like a naked new-born babe . . .'
Images of children, animals and storm combine to emphasize the retribution Macbeth fears will be brought upon him by the forces of Order.

115/153	Order

118   1 7 21 'And Pity, like a naked new-born babe . . .'
Note that Macbeth fears especially the power of the children. Why?

78/126	Children
115/119	Macbeth

119   1 7 25 'That tears shall drown the wind.'
Macbeth recognizes the danger of ambition. Why then does he still proceed with the murder? Macbeth seems fully aware of his own weakness. His great tragedy is that in spite of (or because of) this he gambles everything. Such is the power of ambition. Here Macbeth gives a chilling description of ambition's inner logic. An interesting forward reference at this point is to the imagery of ambition as a horse – compare it with Ross's conversation with the Old Man.

108/123	Ambition
118/120	Macbeth

120   1 7 31 'We will proceed no further . . .'
Macbeth realizes the enormity of the deed he is contemplating, for his sense of justice and loyalty are not at first weak. What happens to change his attitude? Notice here that ironically it is the imagery of clothing which Macbeth uses to describe his new status – clothing as in disguise, conceal-ment and the having of a 'false face'.

Has Duncan been a weak King? After all, he has put up with rebellion and invasion and has not even bothered to lead his own army. But if this is right, why was he so swift and firm in ordering the death of Cawdor? Conversely, what sort of King would allow his generals to make peace terms without consulting him? It is possible that Duncan has been *too* good and that he was unwise to trust so much in others. Whose fault is it that Duncan is now about to be murdered?

116/129	Duncan
119/121	Macbeth

121   1 7 34 'Which would be worn now . . .'
Macbeth sees himself as clothed in other people's good opinions. These are his rightful garments. Lady Macbeth continues Macbeth's metaphor of clothing; he has dressed himself in ambition. Notice how their conversation

98/167	Clothing
120/124	Macbeth

is as revealing by what they do not mention as by what they do. For example, what crucially important influence on them both is not mentioned at all throughout the whole scene? (Hint: Macbeth's letter spoke of little else.)

122   1 7 35 'Was the hope drunk . . .'
Lady Macbeth will develop the ideas of drunken sleep and uncontrollable behaviour later on in the play, during the night of the murder.

34/129	Sleep
103/129	Treachery

123   1 7 39 'Such I account thy love.'
Lady Macbeth's fury at Macbeth's second thoughts shows her obsession with the idea of power. Why must she make Macbeth act quickly?

119/125	Ambition
108/124	Lady Macbeth

124   1 7 46 'I dare do all that may become a man;'
Macbeth will only act honourably. Banquo says something similar in the next scene. There is one person, however, who can turn Macbeth from the path of honour.

123/125	Lady Macbeth
121/126	Macbeth

125   1 7 54 'Does unmake you. I have given suck, . . .'
Lady Macbeth will go to any lengths, and is even willing to overturn natural order, rather than go back on her intention. More than any other writer of his age, Shakespeare seems to have seen the mixture of love and violent death as inevitable.

123/128	Ambition
124/127	Lady Macbeth

126   1 7 54 'Does unmake you. I have given suck, . . .'
It is ironic, and chilling, that Lady Macbeth's melodramatic reference to child-killing is turned into a reality later by Macbeth.

118/208	Children
124/131	Macbeth

127   1 7 56 'I would while it was smiling . . .'
Lady Macbeth's imagery at this point sounds gruesomely like that of the Witches in Act 4.

125/128	Lady Macbeth
104/137	Witches

128   1 7 60 'But screw your courage . . .'
Lady Macbeth still thinks that courage is all that is needed for the murder. Macbeth is not used to conspiracy and does not see the flaws in Lady Macbeth's plan. Is this a weakness in him?

125/165	Ambition
127/130	Lady Macbeth

129   1 7 61 'And we'll not fail. When Duncan . . .'
Sleep is here associated with peace and innocence, but it will be used as a means whereby evil may be perpetrated. Macbeth feels he has murdered sleep when he kills Duncan, and sleep becomes an enemy to both Macbeth and Lady Macbeth.

122/135	Sleep
122/131	Treachery
120/0	Duncan

130   1 7 78 'As we shall make our griefs . . .'
Lady Macbeth finally persuades Macbeth. They both seem to think that 'sound and fury' will protect them from being suspected of Duncan's murder. Lady Macbeth does not seem to have to try too hard to win her husband over. Is he a man who is usually easily swayed? What would certainly have been even more shocking to Shakespeare's audience is the fact that Macbeth deliberately embraces evil – he actually seeks out the Witches later in the play.

128/146	Lady Macbeth
37/163	Noise

131 1 7 82 'False face must hide . . .'
The clothing of innocent appearance must cover the treachery underneath. At the end of this important scene, decide what are the factors that have changed Macbeth's mind. Try to answer the following questions. How far is Lady Macbeth to blame? Could Macbeth have still refused to carry out the murder? If you think he could, why didn't he?

Act 2

132 2 1 1 'How goes the night, boy?'
The suspense builds up. The introduction to the audience of Banquo's son is dramatically important. Think of what the Witches told Banquo: do you know why it is important?

133 2 1 2 'The moon is down; . . .'
There is neither moon nor stars. Complete darkness and evil will now take over the world.

134 2 1 4 'Hold, take my sword.'
Note the charm of Banquo's fatherly chat to his son – it is dark because they are saving (husbanding) on candles in heaven.

135 2 1 6 'A heavy summons lies like . . .'
Banquo is not immune from terrible dreams. We are not told the nature of these 'cursèd thoughts' which plague him. Does he fear for Duncan's life, having perhaps already guessed the way events might go after what the Witches said to Macbeth? Is he struggling with his own ambitions for his children? Banquo here (and Macbeth later) find that sleep no longer brings peace, but Banquo can at least ask God for help – Macbeth cannot, for he cannot say 'Amen'.

136 2 1 8 'Restrain in me the cursèd thoughts . . .'
What are these 'thoughts' that Banquo is trying to reject? Notice how Banquo calls for his sword back again as soon as someone approaches – isn't this supposed to be a friendly castle?

137 2 1 20 ' I dreamt last night of the three . . .'
Banquo is honest enough to admit his thoughts. However Macbeth must now put on 'a false face'.

138 2 1 33 'Is this a dagger which I see . . .'
We see Macbeth, once a fearless soldier, now tormented by images of blood and fear of the unknown. This kind of killing goes against his character; he has to fight his own nature to carry it out. The action is halted for us to absorb this important knowledge. This scene is a dramatic parallel to Lady Macbeth's sleepwalking monologue, but Macbeth imagines the horror in advance. Lady Macbeth's weak powers of imagination conjure up the horror for her too late to save her sanity.

In order to murder Duncan they had to distort their natures and they must then live with the consequences. Macbeth thought that by murder he could become a king but he discovers that all he has been able to become is a murderer.

	Characters and ideas previous/next comment
126/138	Macbeth
129/136	Treachery
114/138	Aspects of style
0/134	Fleance
98/139	Darkness
110/135	Banquo
132/222	Fleance
134/136	Banquo
0/141	Dreams
129/143	Sleep
135/137	Banquo
131/233	Treachery
136/177	Banquo
127/141	Witches
132/162	Aspects of style
131/140	Macbeth

139   2 1 33 'Is this a dagger which I see . . .'
The darkness of night is used for dramatic effect during murders. The darkness of storms is also used in a symbolic way during speeches and at the meetings with the Witches. But there is a more subtle kind of darkness which pervades the play's imagery, the darkness and loneliness of the mind. Macbeth describes this deeper kind of darkness in a short speech of great poignancy: 'I have lived long enough . . .' (see Act 5, scene 3).

133/144   Darkness

140   2 1 33 'Is this a dagger which I see . . .'
Macbeth is much moved by portents – in this case the dagger. This common Elizabethan stage convention was used to depict the tempting (or revealing) of a character with murder in his heart. There are other portents and visions which Macbeth is exposed to in the play, and they are symbolic both of the external (visible) evil of the Witches and the internal (hidden) evil growing in Macbeth.

138/142   Macbeth
95/172   Portents

141   2 1 38 'A dagger of the mind, . . .'
Dreams and visions confuse appearance and reality. Compare Macbeth's attitude here with the remarks he made after his first meeting with the Witches.

135/143   Dreams
137/146   Witches

142   2 1 46 'And, on thy blade and dudgeon, . . .'
As a soldier, Macbeth has been able to kill without fear. Why does the thought of this blood now haunt him?

20/155   Blood
140/144   Macbeth

143   2 1 49 'Thus to mine eyes. Now o'er the one . . .'
Wicked dreams afflict not only Banquo but all mankind. Chaos is spreading in nature as the evil moment approaches.

141/227   Dreams
135/147   Sleep

144   2 1 56 'Moves like a ghost. Thou sure . . .'
Macbeth now feels more comfortable in darkness. He is about to embark upon a journey into evil.

139/149   Darkness
142/145   Macbeth

145   2 2 3 'It was the owl that shrieked, . . .'
Did Lady Macbeth hear the scream of an owl (a night-hunting predator), or of Macbeth, or of Duncan or of the spirits of goodness? Shakespeare often produced telling dramatic moments with the lightest of such touches. Appropriately the owl, a bird of prey which hunts at night, announces the evil deed.

111/172   Animals
144/148   Macbeth

146   2 2 11 'Confounds us. – Hark! – I laid their . . .'
Like the Witches, Lady Macbeth cannot do evil directly, she can act only through others, in this case her husband. Why does Macbeth adopt the same tactic to kill Banquo?

130/147   Lady Macbeth
141/174   Witches

147   2 2 12 'He could not miss 'em'
Lady Macbeth has said that she would be prepared to destroy a child of her own but is here unable to kill the King; yet she abused Macbeth when he seemed unwilling to murder Duncan. What does this tell you about her?

146/149   Lady Macbeth
143/148   Sleep

148   2 2 22 'There's one did laugh in's sleep, . . .'
Sleep represents innocence and peace; Macbeth has murdered them. He is contaminated by evil and cannot ask for blessing. He is terrified by what this implies and suffers the first consequence of his evil act. Notice that the innocent sleepers can pray for peace after their dreams.

145/156   Macbeth
147/151   Sleep

149   2 2 33 'These deeds must not be thought . . .'
Lady Macbeth reveals the darkness growing within her, which will eventually make her insane. Does Macbeth eventually return to reality, and if so, why did the darkness not drive him also to madness? (Or do you think it did?)

144/174   Darkness
147/150   Lady Macbeth

150   2 2 34 'After these ways; so, it will . . .'
It is interesting that it should be Lady Macbeth who first mentions madness. Is she able to avoid thinking about their deeds?

149/157   Lady Macbeth
91/154   Sickness

151   2 2 35 'Methought I heard a voice cry, . . .'
Carefully study this short speech by Macbeth. It highlights the use of the image of sleep to portray innocence killed by evil. Macbeth has also killed his own innocence and 'shall sleep no more', which almost becomes literally true.

148/152   Sleep

152   2 2 39 'Chief nourisher in life's feast.'
Sleep is seen here as related to the imagery of food and the banquet – 'life's feast'.

84/168   Banquet
151/175   Sleep

153   2 2 39 'Chief nourisher in life's feast.'
Sleep and food are essential parts of the natural order of things; study the banquet scene, noting how Macbeth destroys the 'order' of the feast.

117/193   Order

154   2 2 46 'So brain-sickly of things.'
This is Lady Macbeth's second reference to madness in this scene. Unnatural events and deeds are being associated with madness. Banquo wondered about this when he asked '. . . Or have we eaten on the insane root?'.

150/170   Sickness

155   2 2 46 'So brain-sickly of things.'
Lady Macbeth thinks only about the appearance of blood while Macbeth fears for his bloodstained soul. See how this imagery is exploited in the sleepwalking scene.

142/156   Blood
33/158   Water

156   2 2 50 'I'll go no more.'
In battle, Macbeth has seen far worse sights than this. Why, then, is he afraid to look at Duncan's body?

155/158   Blood
148/158   Macbeth

157   2 2 52 'Infirm of purpose!'
Lady Macbeth is not sensitive to the moral dilemma of Macbeth. Did she ever really understand her husband or clearly see the reality of what she has done? The child in its innocence is afraid of what appears evil. Unlike her husband, Lady Macbeth seems unable to recognize the reality of her present situation: the guilt which she attempts to pass to others will eventually destroy her.

55/159   Fear
150/160   Lady Macbeth

158   2 2 60 'Will all great Neptune's ocean . . .'
Water will normally clean (purify) things which are contaminated, but there is not enough to wipe out the stain on Macbeth's soul. Again, the enormity of his crime destroys the natural order of things. Macbeth's image of turning the pure sea to blood is effective literally and symbolically. Lady Macbeth's 'a little water' speech later on is in marked contrast, and highlights their different perceptions of the murder.

156/160	Blood
156/161	Macbeth
155/160	Water

159   2 2 64 'My hands are of your colour; . . .'
Fear is a subtle theme in the play. We find characters afraid of things which at other moments they are unmoved by (Lady Macbeth and blood, blood and Macbeth, Banquo and Macbeth, Macbeth and Macduff, for example). The underlying idea is that people are not afraid of things as such, but of the context in which they occur. Some characters eventually are defeated by their terror (Lady Macbeth), others meet it head on (Macbeth), whilst many (Lady Macduff and the people of Scotland) suffer terror without knowing why.

157/185	Fear

160   2 2 67 'A little water clears us . . .'
Notice the huge gulf between Lady Macbeth's view of events and that of her husband. Both use water imagery but note the truth of Macbeth's vision and the falsity of hers. We might have expected Macbeth (the professional soldier) to be the steadfast one here, not Lady Macbeth. Their attitudes reverse as the play progresses.

158/180	Blood
157/176	Lady Macbeth
158/180	Water

161   2 2 73 'To know my deed 'twere best . . .'
Macbeth would prefer not to think about what he has done and what sort of person this makes him. Has there been a change in his character, or did you expect him to behave like this?

158/165	Macbeth

162   2 3 1 'Here's a knocking indeed!'
Here there is relief from the tension of the previous scene, but it is more than just that. Shakespeare would never allow a drama to slip into melodrama – therefore there must be some change of pace.

138/166	Aspects of style
0/164	Porter

The Porter is almost completely a dramatic device. In so far as he does not actually contribute directly to the action of the play he is almost like a Chorus – a device from Greek tragedy which allowed the audience to be brought up to date with events so far, or prepared for events to come. However, he has a lot to do with the 'pace' of the play and his comedy makes the subsequent revelation of Duncan's murder all the more horrific. There are several other scenes in the play which have a chorus-like quality – can you find them? (Hint: look at the shorter scenes.)

There is more in the Porter scene than at first would appear. During the late medieval age it was traditional that hell was represented as a castle with its gate in the form of a monster's mouth. This tradition stems from the 'Miracle' plays of the time, in which the central character had names like 'Everyman' or 'Man' and the other characters represented common virtues and vices, or angels and devils. These plays always had a strong moral tale to tell, and in them the character of the 'devil-porter' was often an important and comic feature.

163   2 3 1 'Here's a knocking indeed!'
So far in this Act we have seen a considerable number of references to noise, all of them laden with doom. They now reach a climax with a knocking at the door of Macbeth's castle, his 'hell-gate'.

130/229	Noise

	Characters and ideas previous/next comment

164   2 3 1 'Here's a knocking indeed!'
The Porter pretends to be the keeper of hell-gate, a traditional role. Why, in this context, would this be called black humour, that is, a sick joke?

162/166   Porter

165   2 3 4 'Belzebub? Here's a farmer that hanged . . .'
The farmer is ruined because of his ambition. Compare the farmer with Macbeth.

One of the Jesuit conspirators in the Gunpowder Plot was Father Henry Garnet. (See comment 166.) Also in 1605-6 there was a glut of farm produce.

128/197   Ambition
161/167   Macbeth

166   2 3 8 'Faith, here's an equivocator . . .'
Here again is the theme of treachery, but this time as a contemporary allusion to the religious reactionaries who lie under oath in good faith, and still go to Hell. The less educated in the audience could enjoy a laugh at one whose 'cleverness' was his downfall.

This particular joke would have been very topical. Father Henry Garnet (see comment 165) was a conspirator in the Gunpowder Plot and at his arrest he denied all knowledge of it. Later, when he was tricked into admitting his guilt he defended his lies by saying they were not really perjury but were 'equivocation', that is the telling of deliberately misleading half-truths. He argued that this was justified because he was defending his religion. Although the 'equivocation' reference was not wholly made up by Shakespeare (it is implied in the original story in Holinshed) he gave it a very specific focus which was well suited to the time of the play's first performance.

162/188   Aspects of style
164/0   Porter

167   2 3 13 "English tailor come hither for stealing . . .'
The tailor steals fabric. Is there a hint here of Macbeth's 'borrowed robes'?

121/199   Clothing
165/169   Macbeth

168   2 3 22 'Faith, sir, we were carousing till . . .'
When taken to excess even good things can produce disorder, including this 'banquet' of drink.

There is also a much more powerful, subtler echo here, to the Gospel of St Mark, chapter 14, verse 30, where Jesus says to the loyal Peter, 'Truly, I say to you, this very night, before the cock crows twice . . .'. The implications in terms of feasting, treachery and the nature of kingship are closely entwined.

152/179   Banquet
65/170   Chaos

169   2 3 44 'I have almost slipped the hour.'
Time still appears to be on Macbeth's side; had Macduff arrived earlier, Macbeth might have been incriminated straight away.

167/171   Macbeth
112/178   Time

170   2 3 51 'The night has been unruly.'
This list of chaotic events in nature echoes a sickness in the State.

168/173   Chaos
154/184   Sickness

171   2 3 51 'The night has been unruly.'
The storms in nature symbolize the chaos Macbeth has unleashed on the world. Contrast Lennox's amazed tale with Macbeth's brief but telling reply. Notice how, in keeping with the Elizabethan view of the universe as a

169/180   Macbeth
36/192   Storm

whole interlinked creation, disturbances in one part cause disturbances elsewhere – it is therefore quite fitting that the murder of a king is accompanied by screams of death, dire combustion and a feverous and shaking earth.

172   2 3 56 'New-hatched to the woeful time.'
The association of birds of prey with portents of death is re-emphasized. Lennox senses evil, but cannot identify its source.

| 145/193 | Animals |
| 140/190 | Portents |

173   2 3 63 'Confusion now hath made . . .'
The murder of Duncan has unleashed chaos on the world. Duncan was God's choice, and therefore the natural order has been broken.

| 170/175 | Chaos |

174   2 3 68 'Approach the chamber and destroy . . .'
Technically a Gorgon was, according to the Greeks, any one of the three mythical winged monstrous sisters (Stheno, Euryale, and Medusa). They had live snakes for hair, huge teeth and brazen claws. Informally the name is used to describe a fierce or unpleasant woman. Do you think it is only coincidence that Shakespeare has Macduff use this particular image here?

| 149/191 | Darkness |
| 146/202 | Witches |

175   2 3 73 'Shake off this downy sleep, . . .'
The innocence of sleep must face the reality of death. Macbeth has murdered both sleep and innocence.

| 173/179 | Chaos |
| 152/227 | Sleep |

176   2 3 80 'O gentle lady, . . .'
Perhaps Macduff thinks all women are like his 'gentle' wife. This is dramatic irony: the audience already knows Lady Macbeth is an accessory to murder.

| 160/177 | Lady Macbeth |
| 0/182 | Macduff |

177   2 3 85 'Too cruel, anywhere.'
The genuine feeling of Banquo reveals the superficiality of Lady Macbeth's pretence.

| 137/185 | Banquo |
| 176/184 | Lady Macbeth |

178   2 3 88 'Had I but died an hour before . . .'
This speech is very prophetic. Death does become unimportant to Macbeth, and in some senses what he says here may actually have already happened. Is Macbeth just saying these words or do you think he is really speaking from the heart? Is the 'real' Macbeth already 'dead'?

| 69/198 | Fate |
| 169/189 | Time |

179   2 3 92 'The wine of life is drawn, . . .'
This is an image of disorder: imagine a bottle (the image for a State or a person) with no wine (spirit or goodness) left in it but merely the lees (evil or dregs).

| 168/205 | Banquet |
| 175/183 | Chaos |

180   2 3 95 'The spring, the head, the fountain of . . .'
There have always been strong religious connections between wine (mentioned just previously), water and blood. Again the sacrilegious nature of the murder is emphasized. Macbeth links water imagery in a rather gruesome way with that of blood ('fountain of your blood').

160/253	Blood
171/183	Macbeth
160/253	Water

181   2 3 98 'Those of his chamber, as it seemed, . . .'
Lennox seems to draw the conclusion that both Macbeth and Lady Macbeth desire.

| 0/238 | Lennox |

182   2 3 104 'Wherefore did you so?'
Macduff asks a penetrating question. He keeps a cool head and perhaps has made a few deductions.

| 176/281 | Macduff |

183   2 3 110 'And his gashed stabs looked like . . .'
Macbeth knows full well that it is he who has broken the natural order.

| 179/195 | Chaos |
| 180/192 | Macbeth |

184   2 3 116 'Look to the lady!'
Why might it be thought that Lady Macbeth's sudden illness is well timed?

| 177/205 | Lady Macbeth |
| 170/218 | Sickness |

185   2 3 123 'And when we have our naked . . .'
Banquo, as a loyal servant of the Crown, is outraged by this 'bloody piece of work'. What can you deduce from the reactions of Macduff and Macbeth? Banquo has the strength of his faith to help him fight his fear and understand what has happened.

177/202	Banquo
159/216	Fear
71/196	Loyalty

186   2 3 132 'What will you do?'
Malcolm, as the named heir to the Crown, sees at once that he must flee to preserve his safety.

| 70/295 | Malcolm |
| 116/202 | The Crown |

187   2 3 138 'This murderous shaft that's shot . . .'
At this time of chaos no one stands 'upon the order' of their going – they hurry away. It is Macbeth who has initiated this haste.

| 114/198 | Haste |

188   2 4 1 'Threescore and ten I can . . .'
The meeting of the Old Man, Ross and Macduff gives the audience a chance to digest previous events. Ross is used to give a simple, honest reaction to events. Yet the happenings he reports imply chaos in the natural order.

| 166/201 | Aspects of style |

Ross and the Old Man fill in the plot and stress the most terrible aspect of the murder, its unnaturalness. Many of the events they talk about were taken by Shakespeare from Holinshed's account of the murder of King Duff, and it is interesting to compare Shakespeare's treatment with the original:

'For the space of six moneths togither . . . there apeered no sunne by day, nor moone by night in anie part of the realme, but still was the skie covered with continuall clouds, and sometimes such outragious windes arose, with lightenings and tempests, that the people were in great feare of present destruction . . . horsses in Louthian, being of singular beautie and swift-nesse, did eate their owne flesh . . . There was a sparhawke also strangled by an owle.'

189   2 4 1 'Threescore and ten I can . . .'
This kindly Old Man philosophically accepts the various manifestations of time. Notice how he contrasts strongly with Macbeth, for whom time will be an enemy before long.

| 178/207 | Time |

190   2 4 5 'Thou seest the heavens, . . .'
Ross senses the evil atmosphere, but cannot explain its significance. The audience can.

172/231	Portents
54/196	Ross

191   2 4 5 'Thou seest the heavens, . . .'
The murder of Duncan has released the powers of darkness which 'strangle' the light of day. These powers are seen to be gaining in strength.

174/206	Darkness
99/235	Light

192   2 4 5 'Thou seest the heavens, . . .'
Ross describes the upheaval in nature, and in so doing explains the relationship between the actions of Man (who has free will) and the condition of the heavens.

183/194	Macbeth
171/267	Storm

193   2 4 10 ''Tis unnatural, . . .'
The behaviour of animals should reflect the order in nature. Notice the reversal of the 'sparrows and eagles' image as used by the Captain in Act 1, scene 2, when he was reporting the battle to Duncan.

172/194	Animals
153/237	Order

194   2 4 11 'Even like the deed that's done.'
The Old Man and Ross discuss the chaos which now exists within the animal kingdom–the consequences of some terrible deed. Which of the animal images seems to you best to symbolize Macbeth?

193/217	Animals
192/195	Macbeth

195   2 4 14 'And Duncan's horses–a thing . . .'
The horses 'beauteous and swift', are an image of Macbeth 'contending 'gainst obedience'. Like him they have turned 'wild in nature'. This results in the total overthrow of civilized order: 'they ate each other'.

183/237	Chaos
194/206	Macbeth

196   2 4 27 ''Gainst nature still!'
This is an important link in the plot. Ross tells us how the flight of Malcolm and Donalbain has helped Macbeth's story, and incriminated them. But Ross is not a suspicious person and this is only a temporary escape for Macbeth.

185/200	Loyalty
190/200	Ross

197   2 4 28 'Thriftless ambition . . .'
Ross has voiced one of the play's central themes, that of 'thriftless ambition'. Notice his prophetic remark about the consequences of ambition.

165/204	Ambition

198   2 4 31 'He is already named and gone . . .'
Still associated with haste, Macbeth must rush to be crowned, for fear that fate will intervene.

Colmekill, where Duncan's body is taken, is the island of Iona, which was the burial place of Scottish Kings from AD 973 to 1040. Christianity was first introduced into Scotland on Iona in AD 563, by St Columba. Close to St Mary's Abbey, built on Iona by St Columba's followers, is the cemetery where from the 6th century onward fifty-nine kings were buried.

178/219	Fate
187/209	Haste

199   2 4 37 'Well, may you see things well done there– . . .'
Macduff is already concerned at the prospect of Macbeth becoming King. See how the clothing imagery as used here seems to suggest that life under Macbeth (new clothes) may be less comfortable than under Duncan (old clothes).

167/296	Clothing

200   2 4 40 'God's benison go with you, . . .'
The Old Man sees that Ross will always give people the benefit of the doubt.

196/202	Loyalty
196/238	Ross

Act 3

201   3 1 1 'Thou hast it now: . . .'
After the rush of events in the previous Act some time has passed, so that we can see the longer-term effects of Macbeth's actions on himself and others.

188/202	Aspects of style

202   3 1 1 'Thou hast it now: . . .'
Banquo is loyal to the Crown, even when he suspects that it has been gained by foul means. He seems to have no personal ambition for the Crown; the Witches more or less told him simply to wait – his children would be kings, not him. Does this explain Macbeth's haste? This is only a short soliloquy, for, unlike Macbeth, Banquo has no inner turmoil to reconcile. We hear his suspicion of Macbeth, to whom, as King, he has remained loyal. He considers the contents of the Witches' prophecy to him, but only as a possibility. It will not tempt him to evil. Banquo is suspicious of Macbeth, and of the Witches too. Unlike Macbeth, he seems able to resist their temptations, although he does not find it easy. Is it loyalty which keeps Banquo in the service of Macbeth, in spite of his deep suspicions? He appears not to feel himself in any danger. Would you call this a weakness in him?

201/209	Aspects of style
185/203	Banquo
200/204	Loyalty
186/212	The Crown
174/236	Witches

203   3 1 5 'But that myself should be . . .'
Wholesome images of growing plants continue to appear in the play, but no longer in association with Macbeth.

202/204	Banquo
76/213	Growth

204   3 1 6 'Of many kings. If there come truth . . .'
Banquo may have private ambitions of his own. Would his sense of loyalty and what is right, prevent him from giving way to any which he had?

197/209	Ambition
203/207	Banquo
202/301	Loyalty

205   3 1 12 'It had been as a gap in . . .'
Lady Macbeth is still deluding herself that there is some sort of natural order left in their world.

179/237	Banquet
184/223	Lady Macbeth

206   3 1 15 'And I'll request your presence.'
As Macbeth intends that Banquo shall soon be murdered he obviously does not expect to see him at the banquet. Neither does he realize that the spirit world will grant his request in a way he had not expected; this is the emerging pattern for all dealings with the forces or darkness.

191/235	Darkness
195/211	Macbeth

207   3 1 24 'As far, my lord, as will fill . . .'
The guilt-free Banquo sees time as a friend, offering him a leisured day, but Banquo's 'dark hour' is coming soon and he will indeed 'borrow' some time from the world of darkness to haunt Macbeth.

204/210	Banquo
189/221	Time

208   3 1 29 'We hear our bloody cousins . . .'
Does his own mention of Duncan's sons remind Macbeth of the danger from Banquo's son?

126/211   Children

209   3 1 32 'With strange invention.'
Macbeth is almost always in a hurry. This symbolizes his ambition, fuelled by fear. He is trying to go too far, too fast. But at one important point in the play Macbeth's haste vanishes and he seems to waver. Where does this happen, and why is it so significant? (Hint: look at Act 1, scene 7.)

204/215   Ambition
202/224   Aspects
            of style
198/252   Haste

210   3 1 49 'Stick deep; and in his royalty . . .'
Macbeth's assessment of Banquo's character is revealing. How does it match the facts? Can you now make an assessment of Banquo's character?

207/234   Banquo

211   3 1 59 'They hailed him father . . .'
This highlights Macbeth's preoccupation with children and explains why he feels so threatened by them.

208/214   Children
206/212   Macbeth

212   3 1 60 'Upon my head they placed . . .'
The Crown has been achieved through evil means. Macbeth has dressed himself in the trappings of kingship, but the Witches' prophecy to Banquo stops him gaining any satisfaction from it.

211/213   Macbeth
202/259   The Crown

213   3 1 69 'To make them kings, the seeds . . .'
Macbeth is obsessed by potential threats to his security, and the natural growth of Banquo's children is abhorrent to him.

203/214   Growth
212/215   Macbeth

214   3 1 69 'To make them kings, the seeds . . .'
Macbeth here echoes Banquo's use of the word 'seeds' at the meeting with the Witches. Shakespeare's work is rich in the imagery of growth, and he often evokes the idea of the world as a garden. What sort of occupational background do you think most 16th-century people had?

211/228   Children
213/220   Growth

215   3 1 70 'Rather than so, come fate . . .'
Macbeth's battle against fate begins. He will struggle to frustrate the Witches' promises to Banquo. Is he starting to over-reach the limits of his power by setting himself too ambitious a task?

209/256   Ambition
213/216   Macbeth

216   3 1 75 'Have you considered of my speeches?'
Up to the point of Duncan's murder it was Macbeth's own 'steel which smoked with bloody execution'; now that he is plagued by 'daggers of the mind', he uses other 'instruments of darkness' to achieve his ends. Does he think this tactic will free him of guilt?

185/248   Fear
215/218   Macbeth

217   3 1 91 'Ay, in the catalogue ye go . . .'
This is a direct and accurate comparison: there are thoroughbreds and wild dogs in the human race too.

194/225   Animals

218   3 1 106 'Who wear our health but sickly . . .'
Macbeth thinks he can cure his sickness and make things 'perfect' by another murder.

216/219   Macbeth
184/239   Sickness

219   3 1 108 'Whom the vile blows and buffets . . .'
Are the murderers 'shadows' of Macbeth? Do they echo certain aspects of his character in his 'reckless' battle against fate?

198/266	Fate
218/221	Macbeth

---

220   3 1 128 'I will advise you where to plant . . .'
The imagery of planting and growth is reversed; Macbeth prepares the ground for the cutting down of Banquo.

214/226	Growth

---

221   3 1 129 'Acquaint you with the perfect spy . . .'
Macbeth thinks he can manipulate the future, especially if he hurries! Might he have been right? If so, why do you think his plans went wrong?

219/222	Macbeth
207/277	Time

---

222   3 1 134 'Fleance his son, that keeps . . .'
Macbeth is afraid of Fleance, because of the Witches' prophecy. It is just as important to Macbeth that Fleance, as well as his father, dies by the murderers' hands. Macbeth's fears are intensified when Fleance escapes with his life.

Notice how this scene closes with a couplet which echoes that spoken by Macbeth just before he sets out for Duncan's chamber to murder him. There are many such echoes in the play, both in the words spoken and in the use of imagery, and you must be on the lookout for them because they link the different parts of the drama together in a deliberate and revealing way.

134/226	Fleance
221/224	Macbeth

---

223   3 2 5 'Where our desire is got . . .'
Compare Lady Macbeth's state of mind with Macbeth's, both before and after Duncan's murder. What is making her so uneasy now?

Is Lady Macbeth a monster who has led her husband into murder, or is she the ideal wife, encouraging and supporting her husband and helping him to achieve his full potential? What do you think Macbeth's true potential really was – to become a great and noble servant of the Crown, to become the rightful King, or to become a tyrant and a butcherer of women and children?

205/224	Lady Macbeth

---

224   3 2 8 'How now, my lord? Why do you . . .'
Macbeth no longer confides in his wife. Why not? Think about whether you believe the reasons he gives her and whether you think she believes them. Is Macbeth seeking to regain a dominant role after her mastery of events in Act 2? Or is it instead a skilful piece of writing by Shakespeare? After all, if Lady Macbeth had been involved in Banquo's murder she also would have to see his ghost in the banquet scene, and this would have spoiled the effect. It is important that only Macbeth sees Banquo's ghost. Can you think why? (Hint: Lady Macbeth will see her ghosts later.)

223/230	Lady Macbeth
222/225	Macbeth
209/236	Aspects of style

---

225   3 2 13 'We have scorched the snake, . . .'
Notice how Macbeth's animal imagery is always associated with either powerful and aggressive animals or with those of the lower orders. We see from here onwards a particular concentration on the latter. Try to work out what effect this produces, and why this device is so effective.

217/228	Animals
224/230	Macbeth

---

226   3 2 13 'We have scorched the snake, . . .'
Macbeth fears Banquo's children, because the Witches foretold that they would be future Kings, like Duncan's son, Malcolm. Macbeth sees this threat as being like a snake which when damaged or cut will 'close' (join up again).

222/234	Fleance
220/232	Growth

Regeneration and growth are forces which Macbeth constantly fears. The play shows the forces of order recovering from attacks by tyranny and destruction to make the world good again. Is *Macbeth* therefore essentially an optimistic play?

---

227   3 2 18 'In the affliction of these . . .'
Macbeth has murdered sleep and only the dead sleep peacefully. Tormented by dreams, he envies the dead, and now sees death as a peaceful sleep after sickness. The meaning and power of dreams feature clearly in Lady Macbeth's sleepwalking scene. But we also see Banquo cursing the thoughts 'that nature gives way to in repose' (Act 2, scene 1); whilst Macbeth has 'wicked dreams' which 'abuse sleep' (Act 2, scene 1). Macbeth suffers a 'waking dream' when he sees the dagger, and in the banquet scene we see the world of dreams fuse with the world of wakefulness, as Banquo appears as a 'borrower of the night'.

143/260   Dreams
175/245   Sleep

---

228   3 2 36 'O, full of scorpions . . .'
The fact that Banquo and Fleance are alive is poisoning Macbeth's mind. Notice that the animal imagery has now descended to the lower order of beasts.

225/231   Animals
214/236   Children

---

229   3 2 40 'Then be thou jocund.'
Look at how many references to noise are packed into the next few lines. They announce 'a deed of dreadful note', and the unpleasant animal references also lend emphasis to the darkness of the deed.

163/292   Noise

---

230   3 2 45 'Be innocent of the knowledge, . . .'
Why does Macbeth want his wife to be innocent of Banquo's murder? Lady Macbeth has spent quite a while telling us how well she knows her husband, but does he in fact know her character better than she knows his? Macbeth calls upon 'seeling night'. Compare in detail this speech and that of Lady Macbeth ('come thick night . . .'). Consider this complete reversal of roles and what it says about the development of their characters between these speeches.

224/244   Lady Macbeth
225/239   Macbeth

---

231   3 2 51 'And the crow makes wing . . .'
The carrion crow acts as a symbol of death; remember that Macbeth spoke of Banquo's soul in 'flight' at the end of the last scene. The density and freshness of Shakespeare's imagery is one of the marks of his genius.

228/246   Animals
190/0   Portents

---

232   3 2 52 'Good things of day begin . . .'
The essential life force is being sapped from nature. The plant images are unwholesome because growth is being replaced by decay.

226/240   Growth

---

233   3 3 1 'But who did bid thee . . .'
A third murderer arrives! What dramatic reason might there be for this? Is it a spy because Macbeth cannot trust anyone? Is it one of the Witches or even Macbeth himself? If it heightens the drama and tension, does it matter that we don't know? Beware of 'over-interpreting' the play. Remember the plays were written to be watched, not read. Shakespeare's 'inconsistencies' are often never noticed by an audience.

136/274   Treachery

The identity of the third murderer has fascinated scholars for years and as well as the explanations offered above it has been suggested that he represents Destiny or the Devil himself. It does seem unlikely that it could possibly be Macbeth – can you think why? What would happen to the next scene if Macbeth already knew about the escape of Fleance – would it still make sense? Similarly we do not know whether the other murderers in the play are the same as these here. Can you think who the 'other' murderers are in the play? (Hint: 'The Thane of Fife had a wife . . .' – Lady Macbeth.)

234   3 3 1 'But who did bid thee . . .'
Fleance says almost nothing during the play. He seems to be a dramatic device to point up Macbeth's paranoid obsession with children, what they will grow into, and the future. Compare Fleance's role in the play with that of Lady Macduff's son.

| 210/0 | Banquo |
| 226/0 | Fleance |

Compare also Banquo with Macbeth. Was Banquo a good man? If he was, was he as good as Duncan? Look at his speeches; can you find one which could be quoted against him? (Hint: when did he keep silent when he might well have spoken out?)

235   3 3 19 'Who did strike out the light?'
The murder of Banquo extinguishes the last glimmering of light and hope in Macbeth's headlong descent into darkness. Notice the first murderer's poignant mention of the last 'streaks of day'.

| 206/251 | Darkness |
| 191/251 | Light |

236   3 3 20 'There's but one down; . . .'
The escape of Fleance enables the Witches' prophecies to come true. Notice that they never tell an outright lie; the riddles in which they speak are much too subtle for that. Remembering that all Shakespeare's plays are meant to be *seen* and *heard*, can you hear the telling pun in this line? (Hint: see comment 235.)

228/240	Children
202/255	Witches
224/254	Aspects of style

Macbeth is the shortest and swiftest-moving of Shakespeare's tragedies. This is helped by the fact that it has no sub-plot. Even the secondary characters are drawn less clearly in order to concentrate attention on Lord and Lady Macbeth. We are not distracted with incidental background, like who first proposed the murder of Duncan, why the third murderer appears or who they all are, or why Macduff left his family so exposed in Scotland and fled to England, for example. An audience usually does not become distracted by these considerations, but accepts that Macbeth had evil thoughts dormant in his mind before he met the Witches, that a tyrant cannot trust anyone, not even his own hired assassins, and that Macduff was placed in a terrible dilemma.

237   3 4 1 'You know your own degrees, . . .'
This formal banquet is a metaphor; order is essential for the well-being of the kingdom and society. It is important for people to know their place so that disorder may be avoided. Macbeth unconsciously acknowledges this fact. This is a key scene, not merely for the appearance of Banquo's ghost, embodying all Macbeth's fear of retribution, but as a symbol of the disorder of his reign. There is no resemblance to majestic hospitality, just undignified confusion.

205/241	Banquet
195/245	Chaos
193/239	Order

238   3 4 1 'You know your own degrees, . . .'
The only named guests at the banquet, Lennox and Ross, have transferred their unswerving loyalty to Macbeth, to the man they now regard as the legitimate King.

181/257	Lennox
200/284	Ross

239   3 4 20 'Then comes my fit again.'
Macbeth longs for a return to order and security, but all his attempts to achieve it through evil means are frustrated. He sees his fear as a sickness which can be cured, literally at a stroke, but meanwhile he is a prisoner of fate.

230/242	Macbeth
237/241	Order
218/243	Sickness

240   3 4 28 'There the grown serpent lies.'
Macbeth fears the growth of the worm (Fleance) into a dangerous serpent, but puts this worry aside for the moment.

236/270	Children
232/271	Growth

241   3 4 35 'From thence, the sauce to meat . . .'
Lady Macbeth realizes that formality and order are essential to a banquet, and that unseemly disorder is becoming apparent.

237/247	Banquet
239/259	Order

242   3 4 49 'Thou canst not say I did it; . . .'
By denying responsibility for actually murdering Banquo, Macbeth hopes to preserve his appearance of innocence. He obviously fails to convince the ghost. Who then is he really trying to deceive, and why?

Macbeth is shown as being like the murderers he has hired – they have become assassins because their ambitions were thwarted, they were once honourable soldiers but now barely rank as 'men'. Notice how the second murderer's speech ('I am reckless what I do to spite the world') and that of the first ('I would set my life on any chance to mend it or be rid on't) are both echoed by Macbeth's own speeches at the end of the play.

239/248	Macbeth

243   3 4 51 'Gentlemen, rise. His highness . . .'
What is Macbeth actually suffering from?

239/294	Sickness

244   3 4 57 'Feed, and regard him not.'
Lady Macbeth again taunts her husband with cowardice as she did when he (perceptively) had doubts about the wisdom of murdering Duncan. Look at how closely the imagery here shadows that used by Lady Macbeth after Duncan's murder. Notice in the play how slowly Lady Macbeth comes to the realization of their wrong-doing.

This the last time we see Lady Macbeth in control of events or of herself. She seems worn out and instead of chastising Macbeth for his behaviour as she did before the murder, she remarks only that he lacks sleep – ironically so, in view of what she is doing when we meet her next. The scene is in fact the turning point for them both – this is also the last time we see Macbeth's conscience appealing to him through his sense of guilt, and even here he eventually brushes it away.

230/282	Lady Macbeth

245   3 4 70 'If charnel-houses and our graves . . .'
One of the unforeseen consequences of the chaos that Macbeth has unleashed upon the world is that the dead may rise again; even in death there may be no peace.

237/247	Chaos
227/254	Sleep

	Characters and ideas previous/next comment	

246 3 4 98 'What man dare, I dare.'
These animals which Macbeth mentions here all represent forces and threats which he feels competent to deal with–he is a man of action; but, unfortunately, the powers threatening him at this point in the play are spiritual, not physical.

231/263 Animals

247 3 4 108 'You have displaced the mirth, . . .'
Read these two lines and remember that the banquet is a metaphor: Macbeth's great banquet is over, in more senses than one.

241/249 Banquet
245/249 Chaos

248 3 4 111 'Without our special wonder?'
Why is it that only Macbeth can see the ghost? What preserves the others who are present from seeing it?

216/250 Fear
242/250 Macbeth

249 3 4 117 'Question enrages him. At once, . . .'
Lady Macbeth presides over the breaking up of the banquet–the only time when Macbeth's kingship might have had a form of ceremonial recognition.

This is a key scene in the play and represents the major turning point for Macbeth and his wife. It closes the first half of the action, in which we see Macbeth's relentless rise to power and at the same time provides the occasion on which we see him betray himself–the occasion on which his power begins to slip through his fingers and the second half of the action begins.

247/261 Banquet
247/267 Chaos

250 3 4 121 'It will have blood, they say; . . .'
Macbeth fears retribution, and that his blood will be shed in revenge for Banquo's death. He sees that he cannot now avoid being exposed for what he is.

248/285 Fear
248/252 Macbeth

251 3 4 126 'Almost at odds with morning, . . .'
At this point in the action of the play, of what could this conflict between darkness and light be symbolic? (Hint: study the last few references to darkness and light.)

235/262 Darkness
235/322 Light

252 3 4 133 'More shall they speak, . . .'
Impatient to know what is to come, Macbeth determines to seek out the Witches.

209/280 Haste
250/253 Macbeth

253 3 4 135 'All causes shall give way.'
In this famous speech Macbeth's use of water imagery reaches its most telling, echoing the Captain's 'Golgotha' speech in Act 1. Just as Macbeth feared in his speech in Act 2 (just after the Porter), the 'fairness' of water has now become mixed with the 'foulness' of spilled blood. Macbeth's journey into the sea of blood has left him so deeply committed to the powers of evil, that he resolves that it will be better to hold his course through the coming storm. Decide whether you think he is right. Could he retreat from here back to where he once was, or is his fate now sealed?

180/300 Blood
252/256 Macbeth
180/323 Water

254 3 4 140 'You lack the season . . .'
The important function of sleep in nature is emphasized here–but who was responsible for its destruction? This line is a good example of one theme being woven into the rich imagery of the whole play; there are many others

245/260 Sleep
236/255 Aspects of style

and you should try to listen for them as you read or watch the drama.

This scene contains a quite remarkable telescoping of time, made all the more admirable by the way audiences never seem to notice it. The banquet must happen fairly soon after Duncan's murder, because news has only just arrived about where Malcolm and Donalbain have fled to. Yet by the end of the scene Macbeth has established a complete network of spies throughout the land and by scene six we have Lennox talking about 'our suffering country, under a hand accursed!' as though Macbeth were a well-established tyrant.

For a play so full of battles, murders, fleeing people, negotiations in foreign lands and geographical switches of place, it is remarkable that we concentrate so much on the emotional and psychological states of the main characters, and are not distracted by all the action.

---

255   3 5 1 'Why, how now, Hecat?'
This is an interesting scene, because it prepares the audience for Macbeth's downfall, with the intervention of Hecat. Hitherto Macbeth has thought he was using the Witches; now they will use him for their devilish enjoyment.

In folklore Hecat was the Goddess of the Moon, as well as of Witches – hence the reference to 'pale Hecat'.

This scene is generally thought not to be by Shakespeare, and is omitted in some editions of the play.

209/257	Aspects of style
236/262	Witches

---

256   3 5 13 'Loves for his own ends, . . .'
Hecat says Macbeth is not a true lover of evil; it is ambition which has made him evil. How accurate do you think this is?

215/362	Ambition
253/265	Macbeth

---

257   3 6 1 'My former speeches have but hit . . .'
In a speech heavy with irony, the previously loyal Lennox shows that even the least suspicious of Macbeth's nobles are now aware of his tyranny and crimes.

This scene is another example of a kind of Chorus. The unnamed Lord represents the Scottish nobles just as the Old Man represented the ordinary people.

255/258	Aspects of style
238/331	Lennox

---

258   3 6 24 'The son of Duncan, . . .'
Minor characters such as this Lord are, like Lennox and Ross, often used to summarize the action at various points in the play, or to bring the audience up to date with important events. This particular instance is a good example.

257/262	Aspects of style

---

259   3 6 24 'The son of Duncan, . . .'
One of the Lords here expresses hopes for the future, emphasizing the proper characteristics required for kingship and its divine source.

241/261	Order
212/273	The Crown

---

260   3 6 34 'Give to our tables meat, . . .'
A return is desired to the situation where 'these terrible dreams which shake us nightly' are no more, and sleep becomes again 'the season of all natures'.

227/321	Dreams
254/272	Sleep

261   3 6 35 'Free from our feasts and banquets . . .'
Daggers and knives are associated with foul deeds. The lord speaks for the
State, which desires the return of its 'feasts and banquets' to order. Contrast
this with Macbeth's banquet.

249/349	Banquet
259/283	Order

Act 4

262   4 1 1 'Thrice the brinded cat hath mewed.'
The Witches set Macbeth on the path of evil. Now they make sure he will
continue. The atmosphere is full of images of evil and danger. Compare this
scene with the first meeting of Macbeth and the Witches. The Witches
exercise supernatural control over fate and time by the use of magic. But
mankind has free will, and so the powers of darkness can triumph only with
his help.

This reappearance of Hecat is thought to be an insertion, not Shakespeare's
original work. Look also at comment 255.

258/280	Aspects of style
251/264	Darkness
255/264	Witches

263   4 1 5 'In the poisoned entrails throw: . . .'
The animal imagery now works at its lowest level; references to bits of
animals and a disgusting assortment of other ingredients prepare a suitable
atmosphere for the entry of Macbeth, and show the Witches in all their true
foulness.

246/283	Animals

264   4 1 44 'By the pricking of my thumbs, . . .'
The Witches recognize the coming of a kindred spirit. Were they also able to
do this at the start of the play?

262/265	Darkness
262/278	Witches

265   4 1 47 'How now, you secret, black, . . .'
Macbeth addresses the Witches in an almost 'familiar' way, very different
from his response earlier in the play. Why is this? Note how completely they
are identified with darkness.

Macbeth is now a king who places his faith not in God but in the forces of
darkness. This would have been even more shocking in Shakespeare's day,
because of the emphasis his society placed upon the 'natural' order of the
universe.

264/268	Darkness
256/267	Macbeth

266   4 1 49 'I conjure you, . . .'
In this outburst Macbeth demands to know what fate has in store for him,
and with this incantation forces the Witches to show him the future.

219/287	Fate

267   4 1 51 'Though you untie the winds . . .'
Macbeth does not care what chaos is unleashed, he will know the future
from the Witches. Do you think he realizes that his images of storm and
tempest are his prophecy of the future? In this powerful imagery Macbeth
unwittingly forsees the chaos that is about to be unleashed in nature and on
the State (by whom?). Macbeth's use of the word 'conjour' is interesting in
this context – does Lady Macbeth ever play a similar scene? (Hint: Check Act
1, scene 5.)

249/284	Chaos
265/268	Macbeth
192/277	Storm

268   4 1 62 'Call 'em. Let me see 'em.'
The initiative has been taken by Macbeth. It is his decision to visit the
Witches and it is he who summons the Witches' masters. But he has no
control over them; he is told to listen and say nothing.

265/325	Darkness
267/269	Macbeth

269   4 1 70 'Macbeth, Macbeth, Macbeth, . . .'
The spirits of darkness hide truth in the ambiguous way in which they say
things. Macbeth's willingness to trust his future to their prophecies will be
used to destroy him; remember Banquo's remark on their first meeting with
the Witches.

The Apparitions know his thoughts and although Macbeth probably thinks
that the 'Armed Head' is Macduff, we see that at the end of the play it is
Macbeth's head which is cut off.

268/273	Macbeth
60/270	Prophecy

270   4 1 75 *Thunder. Second Apparition, a Bloody Child*
Two of the three Apparitions the Witches call are children; appropriately the
first is Lady Macduff's son and the second is Malcolm. Children are
represented in the play as symbols of natural order and growth, and are
therefore a major concern of Macbeth's throughout much of the play.

240/271	Children
269/274	Prophecy

271   4 1 78 'Be bloody, bold, and resolute; . . .'
This carefully worded reassurance seeks to allay Macbeth's deep-seated fear
of the threat he sees in children, and what they may grow into. To what
extent is Macbeth deluding himself, or are the Witches deliberately trying to
lead him to the wrong conclusions? Why do they not just tell him an outright
lie? (Think about whether the play would be as good if they did.)

270/275	Children
240/319	Growth

272   4 1 85 'And sleep in spite of thunder.'
Macbeth continues to make reference to the fact that the peace of sleep
eludes him, yet he still insists that one more murder will solve all his
problems.

260/321	Sleep

273   4 1 85 'What is this . . .'
The Apparitions show Macbeth that his hold on the crown is temporary.

269/275	Macbeth
259/276	The Crown

274   4 1 89 'Be lion-mettled, proud, . . .'
Macbeth is desperate to be reassured about his future. The Apparitions
exploit this; they tell no lies but present the truth in such a way as to give
Macbeth false hope and lead him towards his destruction. Why do they do
this?

270/315	Prophecy
233/289	Treachery

275   4 1 99 'To time and mortal custom.'
Macbeth's paranoia about children can be controlled no longer. The
succession to the Crown is a matter which obsesses him. He demands to see
the future and finds his worst fears realized.

271/288	Children
273/276	Macbeth

276   4 1 112 'Thy crown does sear mine eye-balls.'
Macbeth now finds it painful to look at the crown, and this is also true for the
other objects described using imagery of gold and purity. Like all spirits of
darkness he begins to shun the light, the heavenly and all things pure.

275/277	Macbeth
273/301	The Crown

The balls and sceptres symbolize the union of the crowns of England and Scotland and so what is seen in the glass is James I himself and his line. This must have been a wonderfully effective scene when played in the presence of the King and his court, especially if it was indeed played at Hampton Court (see comment 16). The representation of the eight Stuart Kings would have linked the reign of Macbeth and James I in a powerful way.

	Characters and ideas previous/next comment

277   4 1 116 'What, will the line stretch out . . .'
Macbeth once thought himself to be the master of time. Now the future seems to have rushed out of his control. Had he always misunderstood the situation or has something (someone?) intervened to ruin his plans? If so, what or who is it? Scotland is described in images of noise and storms – as Macbeth foresaw in scene 1.

276/278   Macbeth
267/286   Storm
221/287   Time

278   4 1 124 'Ay, sir, all this is so.'
The Witches would seem to be mocking Macbeth now that their evil charms have worked. Notice the irony in their reference to 'this great king'.

277/279   Macbeth
264/279   Witches

279   4 1 137 'Infected be the air whereon . . .'
Macbeth has taken until now to begin fully appreciating the nature of the Witches. What do you think blinded him for so long?

278/280   Macbeth
278/346   Witches

280   4 1 145 'Unless the deed go with it.'
His soliloquies mark the major phases in the steady deterioration of Macbeth's character. Now he seems to have lost all vestige of conscience. Time is running ahead of Macbeth's actions but he thinks he can counter this by moving even faster! Macbeth resolves to become again the man who acts at once without thinking too much about it. The Witches have removed his fear, but he now seems to want to pursue his murderous course to the most extreme limits.

262/291   Aspects of style
252/340   Haste
279/294   Macbeth

281   4 2 1 'What had he done to make him fly . . .'
We never see Macduff and his Lady together, unlike Macbeth and his Lady (with whom they are useful comparisons). What can you learn about the two men by studying their very different reactions to the deaths of their wives? In her fear, Lady Macduff accuses her husband of folly or cowardice. What are her true opinions of him, as shown just before the murder?

94/282   Lady Macduff
182/295   Macduff

282   4 2 6 'Wisdom! To leave his wife, . . .'
The gentle love of Lady Macduff for her family, and her concern with right and wrong, are in violent contrast with the single-minded desire for power shown by Lady Macbeth when we first meet her.

244/290   Lady Macbeth
281/290   Lady Macduff

283   4 2 9 'He wants the natural touch; . . .'
Compare the ugly animal imagery used by Macbeth with Lady Macduff's allusion to the wren; the weak will fight the strong when their cause is righteous.

263/288   Animals
261/293   Order

284   4 2 18 'But cruel are the times . . .'
Ross is now fully aware of the effects of tyranny; he sees that he, like many others, has almost unconsciously been acting out of confusion and fear. Is this is a general truth about tyranny, do you think?

267/290   Chaos
238/317   Ross

	Characters and ideas previous/next comment

285 4 2 20 'From what we fear, yet know not . . .'
Fear has unpredictable influences on the actions of people. As well as Macduff, have other characters behaved in the ways described here?

250/0   Fear

286 4 2 21 'But float upon a wild . . .'
The unpredictable violence of the sea is again used as a metaphor to illustrate the danger of uncontrolled force. The powerful forces of nature must be kept in balance, if chaos is to be avoided. Macbeth, however, has insufficient moral strength to steer the ship of State through the stormy seas of time.

277/348   Storm

287 4 2 24 'Things at the worst will cease . . .'
Find 'time and the hour runs through the roughest day' (Act 1, scene 3). Notice that the sentiment here is the same, and listen for a further echo of this message of hope for the future expressed, significantly, by Malcolm at the end of this Act. Macbeth, however, would not trust in fate; he tried instead to control the future.

266/320   Fate
277/339   Time

288 4 2 33 'As birds do, mother.'
In the next few lines the freedom of the birds introduces a new aspect of the animal imagery; freedom is linked with the innocent trust of childhood.

283/357   Animals
275/318   Children

289 4 2 45 'Was my father a traitor, . . .'
Consider the definitions of treachery given here and see if you can accurately apply them to any character in the play.

274/353   Treachery

290 4 2 74 'I have done no harm.'
Lady Macduff's words are apt, for where now are Duncan and Banquo? Were these two men's misjudgments really 'folly'? Or was it impossible for them to have foreseen events? Lady Macduff understands that tyranny upsets the natural order of morality. Consider which character does 'harm' and gains by it and which character suffers because of his own goodness?

284/336   Chaos
282/321   Lady Macbeth
282/0   Lady Macduff

291 4 3 1 'Let us seek out some desolate shade, . . .'
This is a very important scene, reintroducing Malcolm and showing, in the subtle dialogue between Malcolm and Macduff, the suspicion and mistrust caused by tyranny. The ideal of kingship is shown in the integrity of Malcolm and the saintliness of the English King. Again, Shakespeare keeps the audience in suspense, this time before the final confrontation.

This scene is important in resuming the drive of the action of the play – after all, we have not seen Malcolm or Macduff for quite a while and they are the two main agents in the forces against Macbeth. Shakespeare paints a very black picture of Macbeth and then tactfully goes on to flatter James I, his own King.

280/304   Aspects of style

292 4 3 5 'New widows howl, new orphans cry, . . .'
This is an echo of the 'lamentings heard i'the air – strange screams of death' heard by Lennox at the time of Duncan's murder.

229/316   Noise

293   4 3 5 'New widows howl, new orphans cry, . . .'
Here we see in detail the dreadful conditions into which people fall in a State without the blessing of order.

283/297   Order
115/307   The State

---

294   4 3 12 'This tyrant, whose sole name . . .'
Macbeth is now so thoroughly associated with evil that his name alone seems sufficient to cause sickness.

280/300   Macbeth
243/314   Sickness

---

295   4 3 14 'He hath not touched you yet.'
The fear bred of tyranny makes Malcolm suspicious of Macduff's motives in coming to England, and rightly so – after all, Macduff was once a friend of Macbeth and he has not been hurt by him so far. Ironically, Macduff's leaving of his wife and children is now taken to imply that he is not worried about their safety!

281/298   Macduff
186/298   Malcolm

---

296   4 3 23 'Though all things foul would . . .'
Foul things tend to put on the borrowed clothes of goodness.

199/333   Clothing

---

297   4 3 24 'Yet grace must still look so.'
Because evil may take the form of goodness this does not mean that true goodness (order) is weakened or diminished in value.

293/299   Order

---

298   4 3 26 'Why in that rawness left you . . .'
The fact that Macduff left his wife and children behind seems to prove to Malcolm that he is in league with Macbeth. Think about why Macduff left his family and whether the reasons are to do with moving the action of the play along, and whether they fit in well with his character. Was Macduff loyal to Duncan? Is he loyal to Malcolm, to his country, to his family? Given that he ran away to England, is he a coward?

295/303   Macduff
295/299   Malcolm

---

299   4 3 39 'I think our country sinks . . .'
Malcolm discusses the importance of order, and we learn that he represents order and moderation. The play ends with a return to order, as appropriately summarized by Malcolm, who has the last speech.

298/301   Malcolm
297/307   Order

---

300   4 3 40 'It weeps, it bleeds, and each . . .'
Has Macbeth fulfilled the Captain's prophetic remark that 'they meant to bathe in reeking wounds or memorise another Golgotha'?

253/327   Blood
294/308   Macbeth

---

301   4 3 45 'When I shall tread upon . . .'
In this long conversation with Macduff, Malcolm tests his friend's loyalty by pretending to be wicked and to have none of the 'graces' of a king. From the way the scene develops we learn that Malcolm is in every respect the rightful heir to the crown. Will he be less easily betrayed than his father? This great test of Macduff's loyalty is understandable; look at things from Malcolm's point of view and remember that Macduff was present at the night of Duncan's murder. Malcolm places a higher value on loyalty now than he did even at the start of the play.

204/302   Loyalty
299/303   Malcolm
276/305   The Crown

---

302   4 3 50 'It is myself I mean; . . .'
Loyalty is an important theme in the play, and both Duncan and Malcolm

301/307   Loyalty

value it a great deal. But loyalty is not just a matter of serving the King come what may. Malcolm tests Macduff on this very point. The dangers of a tyrant becoming the head of state are graphically outlined in *Macbeth*. Loyalty must be to the State, and to the idea of Order, not just to the person who happens to be King (although for the most part it was assumed that the King was there by divine will). To Elizabethans this was an extremely important idea.

---

303   4 3 50 'It is myself I mean; . . .'
From now on Malcolm presents Macduff with the conundrum of 'fair is foul and foul is fair'.

298/305	Macduff
301/311	Malcolm

---

304   4 3 60 'That has a name. But there's . . .'
Where else in the play can we find a scene which is preoccupied with the base behaviour of man when he indulges his sexual appetites? (Hint: 'Here's a knocking indeed!') Does this structural echo form a useful dramatic link? Can you find any other 'bridges' like this in the play?

Notice how the issue of what is real and what is only appearance rises again here. This apparent contradiction (or paradox) runs through the play and is seen here in the testing of Macduff.

291/324	Aspects of style

---

305 4 3 66 'Boundless intemperance . . .'
Macduff is loyal to the Crown, and seems prepared to make considerable allowances for Malcolm's confessed weaknesses, because he is the rightful heir. Malcolm is, of course, testing Macduff, but by this clever device we can be shown how truly good Malcolm is when (later in this scene) he rejects everything he has told Macduff, and goes on to list all his virtues. No wonder Macduff ends up a little baffled!

303/307	Macduff
301/306	The Crown

---

306   4 3 70 'To take upon you what is yours.'
Macduff seems to imply that promiscuity and avarice are not an absolute bar to kingship provided other virtues are present. Is this the road down which Macbeth was tempted?

305/308	The Crown

---

307   4 3 90 'But I have none.'
Malcolm tests Macduff to the limit, by saying that he has none of the qualities that a rightful king should have. Macduff's response a few lines further on reveals that he is so loyal to the Crown that he would sacrifice the proper heir if he was unworthy. (This approach resolved the problem of deposing an 'unfit' king, like Macbeth.) Macduff is a powerful symbol of order in the play, and it is doubly appropriate that it is therefore he who finally kills Macbeth. (If it is *doubly* important what is the other reason?)

302/365	Loyalty
305/318	Macduff
299/309	Order
293/309	The State

---

308   4 3 91 'The king-becoming graces, . . .'
Malcolm lists the 'king-becoming graces'. Consider each in turn and measure Macbeth's character against them. Do not assume that Macbeth's character is unchanging throughout the play (picture him at the start, and then at the end).

300/310	Macbeth
306/313	The Crown

---

309   4 3 97 'Acting it many ways.'
Malcolm, in testing Macduff, describes the total overthrow of all the elements which are the essence of an ordered State.

307/326	Order
307/311	The State

---

310   4 3 97 'Acting it many ways.'
Does Malcolm's description of his worst imaginings serve as a summary of Macbeth's progress to date?

308/312   Macbeth

---

311   4 3 115 'Macduff, this noble passion, . . .'
In testing Macduff, Malcolm reveals that he is truly fit to be heir to the throne and guardian of the State. This is particularly clear in the long speech he makes here, just before the entry of the Doctor. In describing all the terrible things he pretends he would do, he outlines what, in effect, Macbeth has already done to Scotland.

303/312   Malcolm
309/0   The State

---

312   4 3 120 'From over-credulous haste.'
Malcolm will not hurry; haste is dangerous when you need time to think. Contrast this with Macbeth's constant haste.

310/314   Macbeth
311/313   Malcolm

---

313   4 3 122 'I put myself to thy . . .'
Malcolm reveals his true character to be one full of kingly qualities and in this speech proceeds to list them. Be familiar with them, for they will help you to understand the reasons for much of the action of the play.

312/367   Malcolm
308/326   The Crown

---

314   4 3 141 'Ay, sir. There are a crew . . .'
The Doctor describes the healing powers of this good, English king. Contrast this with Macbeth's inability to cure the sickness in himself.

James I, Shakespeare's king, carried on this practice of attempting to heal the sick by touching them (admittedly in a modified form) even though he thought it superstition. It is thought that he did this because others regarded it as evidence of his rightful claim to the throne.

312/332   Macbeth
294/329   Sickness

---

315   4 3 157 'He hath a heavenly gift . . .'
The English king's power comes from heaven, whereas Macbeth listened to the prophecies of evil spirits. Who has the stronger gift of prophecy? Or is the difference one of alignment, rather than of power?

274/338   Prophecy

---

316   4 3 165 'Almost afraid to know itself!'
The noise and turmoil in the State reflect the condition of Macbeth's mind, which also seems 'almost afraid to know itself'.

292/352   Noise

---

317   4 3 204 'Your castle is surprised, . . .'
Once again Ross is a messenger, this time bringing dramatically important news, since Macduff's rage will lead to Macbeth's death.

284/331   Ross

---

318   4 3 215 'He has no children.'
Macduff is in a state of shock – his wife and children have been murdered. His thoughts rapidly turn to revenge, which in Elizabethan times was thought to be a noble and 'manly' sentiment.

288/0   Children
307/359   Macduff

---

319   4 3 237 'Is ripe for shaking, . . .'
The seeds planted by the Witches have grown to fruition – they are 'ripe for shaking' and Macduff desires to be the harvester.

271/337   Growth

320   4 3 239 'The night is long that . . .'
Malcolm knows that the wheel of fate is turning. Notice the similarity between his comment here and one Macbeth makes after his first meeting with the Witches (Act 1, scene 3).

287/339   Fate

Act 5

321   5 1 1 'I have two nights watched . . .'
At this point Lady Macbeth seems unperturbed by the dreams and disturbed sleep which seem to trouble other characters in the play, especially Macbeth and Banquo. Eventually however, the 'terrible dreams' which shook Macbeth are visited upon her in full force, and she then spends her nights suspended in the spirit world of darkness, guilt and madness. The Doctor says 'her eyes are open', but the gentlewoman knows that 'their sense are shut'. The point is, how true has this been all along? Up until now we have always seen Lady Macbeth as apparently able to dismiss from her mind the things that have tormented Macbeth's sleep. Now these same things deny her sleep, which she admitted was 'the season of all nature' (Act 3, scene 4).

260/0   Dreams
290/322 Lady Macbeth
272/328 Sleep

322   5 1 21 'How came she by that light?'
Lady Macbeth seems now to fear the darkness and seeks the security of light.

321/323 Lady Macbeth
251/0   Light

323   5 1 27 'What is it she does now?'
Remember 'a little water clears us of this deed'? Compare the two parts of the play and notice how Shakespeare has skilfully used each of them to heighten the other's dramatic effect.

322/325 Lady Macbeth
253/0   Water

324   5 1 31 'Yet here's a spot.'
Lady Macbeth's speeches in this scene are not true soliloquies, because others are listening, but they serve the same purpose of giving the audience insight into a character: here into a character's subconscious mind. At this stage in the play they serve the structural purpose of completing the story of Lady Macbeth. Her mental disorder also epitomizes the disintegration of Macbeth's court.

The spot that Lady Macbeth cannot remove is the equivalent of the Devil's mark which was supposed to be found on all witches.

304/330 Aspects
         of style

325   5 1 35 '. . . then, 'tis time to do't.'
Lady Macbeth is in her own private hell. Contrast her mental state here with her firmness of purpose and certainty of mind at the time of Duncan's murder. Where did this murkiness, this 'fog and filthy air', first begin? When you think about this question, remember that this imagery is also an analogy for the clouding of the mind, which many characters in the play suffer from to a greater or lesser degree. One of the play's most powerful (and modern!) arguments is that hell is not a place, but a state of mind.

268/0   Darkness
323/328 Lady Macbeth

326   5 1 36 '. . . fie! A soldier and afeard?'
Up until now Lady Macbeth has always insisted that possessing the crown would give them absolute power, but she forgot that the Crown also imposes duties and obligations which Heaven will insist are fulfilled.

309/332 Order
313/337 The Crown

Absolute, divine power exacts a toll on the vessel through which it flows. 'Base' material cannot contain such a spirit without being broken.

327 5 1 48 'Here's the smell of the blood still.'
The evil of her deed has pervaded all Lady Macbeth's senses. Wherever she turns there is now no peace.

300/334	Blood

328 5 1 55 'This disease is beyond my practice; . . .'
The Doctor is aware that things may not be as they appear and that this is not a simple illness. Does the sleepwalking scene show repentance on the part of Lady Macbeth? Is the doctor really suggesting that it may still be possible for her to 'die holily'?

325/329	Lady Macbeth
321/0	Sleep

329 5 1 70 'More needs she the divine . . .'
The illness of Lady Macbeth is not physical. She is now suffering the tempest unleashed by the 'unnatural deeds' that have been committed. Assess her part in these deeds and see if you can identify where her guilt lies.

328/342	Lady Macbeth
314/336	Sickness

330 5 2 1 'The English power is near, . . .'
In this and the next three scenes the action cuts (as in a film) from side to side, until the opponents meet in the final scene. Notice how a lot of the final battle takes place off stage. Why do you think Shakespeare arranged events this way?

324/342	Aspects of style

331 5 2 1 'The English power is near, . . .'
Lennox has now joined the Scottish faction against Macbeth. Ross will appear with Malcolm's army from England.

257/0	Lennox
317/365	Ross

332 5 2 14 'Do call it valiant fury; . . .'
There is a fine dividing line between 'valiant fury' and madness; the former is pictured by the Captain at the start of the play. The State depends for its continued existence on man being able to control his passions; this is central to the whole Elizabethan idea of order.

314/333	Macbeth
326/366	Order

333 5 2 15 'He cannot buckle his distempered . . .'
Macbeth's cause is 'distempered' (diseased), it is not subject to 'the belt of rule' – the ordered nature of a State in harmony with itself and with heaven. Again, we find the image of clothes that cannot be made to fit.

296/335	Clothing
332/334	Macbeth

334 5 2 17 'His secret murders sticking . . .'
All along Macbeth has feared that it would not be possible to evade the responsibility for his deeds, to clean his hands. Angus confirms that this is so.

327/0	Blood
333/338	Macbeth

335 5 2 20 'Nothing in love. Now does . . .'
Macbeth was given the robes of Cawdor, not the robes of a king. The kingly robes he stole from Duncan can only be worn with divine approval. They do not fit Macbeth.

333/341	Clothing

Characters and ideas previous/next comment

	Characters and ideas previous/next comment

336   5 2 27 'Meet we the medicine . . .'
The sickness of the State is about to be purged by the forces of order. The forces of chaos are about to be defeated.

290/0	Chaos
329/343	Sickness

337   5 2 30 'To dew the sovereign flower . . .'
The seed sown by the Witches is about to be overwhelmed by the purity of water, which will release the State from evil. The Crown, 'the sovereign flower', will flourish once more.

319/344	Growth
326/344	The Crown

338   5 3 1 'Bring me no more reports; . . .'
Read this speech carefully. Macbeth is desperately clinging to false hopes but fear is in his mind.

334/340	Macbeth
315/346	Prophecy

339   5 3 20 'When I behold – . . .'
Time is overtaking Macbeth. His fate will soon be decided. He has no control over either.

320/351	Fate
287/350	Time

340   5 3 22 'I have lived long enough: . . .'
The promise of Duncan to 'make thee full of growing' has been frustrated by Macbeth's impatience. By blindly plunging after things of short-lived value he has denied himself the fruits which all good men may harvest in the autumn of life.

280/351	Haste
338/341	Macbeth

341   5 3 32 'I'll fight till from my bones . . .'
Macbeth is anxious to wear his accustomed armour. What does this imply? (Hint: Remember 'borrowed robes'.)

335/355	Clothing
340/342	Macbeth

342   5 3 38 'As she is troubled with . . .'
The roles are reversed. Lady Macbeth is suffering turmoil in her mind whilst her husband is decisive and firm of purpose. In what ways does this echo the start of the play? Is the play 'symmetrical' in construction?

329/369	Lady Macbeth
341/347	Macbeth
330/345	Aspects of style

343   5 3 40 'Canst thou not minister . . .'
The nature of Lady Macbeth's sickness is recognized.

336/345	Sickness

344   5 3 41 'Pluck from the memory . . .'
A diseased plant must be plucked from the garden like a weed. This garden metaphor is also used with reference to the State and the 'sovereign flower' of the Crown.

337/368	Growth
337/0	The Crown

345   5 3 50 'Come, sir, dispatch.'
The doctor can no more cure Lady Macbeth's mental illness than he can the sickness Macbeth thinks is represented by the English in Scotland. Only Macbeth's death will get rid of the English, in the same way that only Lady Macbeth's death will cure her illness. One of the play's themes is the way Macbeth and Lady Macbeth discover that the confusion between what is real and what is imaginary extends to their own actions and thoughts, as here, where Lady Macbeth's illness and sleepwalking are blurred together – as Macbeth says later 'Life's but a walking shadow'.

343/0	Sickness
342/347	Aspects of style

<table>
<tr><td></td><td>Characters and ideas
previous/next comment</td></tr>
</table>

346 5 4 4 'Let every soldier hew him . . .'
The Witches did not lie; their prophecies are being fulfilled, but not in the way that Macbeth assumed. Who therefore is most to blame for his destruction?

338/353 Prophecy
279/0   Witches

347 5 5 9 'I have almost forgot the taste . . .'
Carefully compare this soliloquy with Macbeth's speech 'present fears are less than horrible imaginings' (Act 1, scene 3). Note the change in Macbeth. He has stopped thinking of the future and looks back (perhaps with sorrow) into his past.

345/369 Aspects of style
342/348 Macbeth

348 5 5 10 'The time has been my senses . . .'
Compare this with the shriek heard at the murder of Duncan. Macbeth cannot now be frightened either by his own horrors or the tempests of nature. He has become the eye of the storm. From this still centre of terror Macbeth's words reach out to us over the centuries: 'Life's but a walking shadow, . . .'. Macbeth's chilling conclusion touches one of mankind's greatest, subconscious fears about his life on earth, that 'It is a tale told by an idiot, full of sound and fury, signifying nothing'.

347/349 Macbeth
286/355 Storm

349 5 5 13 'As life were in't.'
There has been no gracious ceremony of kingship for Macbeth; since the appearance of Banquo's ghost, he has 'supped full with horrors'.

261/0   Banquet
348/350 Macbeth

350 5 5 17 'She should have died hereafter.'
This is the climax of Macbeth's unsuccessful fight to conquer time. This is the speech of a man in despair, whom one must pity. Without faith or hope, he says, what is life but a charade? What could you find to say in defence of Lady Macbeth?

349/354 Macbeth
339/354 Time

351 5 5 19 'Tomorrow, and tomorrow, and . . .'
The man of speed and action now bitterly recognizes that in spite of all his efforts to run ahead of time he cannot escape its 'petty pace'.

339/362 Fate
340/0   Haste

352 5 5 26 'And then is heard no more.'
Whose actions in the play could be accurately described as 'full of sound and fury, signifying nothing'? (See also comment 348.)

316/0   Noise

353 5 5 42 'I pull in resolution, . . .'
Macbeth begins to see the tricks behind the Witches' prophecies. Notice how the scene begins with Macbeth confident in the strength of his castle but ends with him abandoning it. Macbeth is making the Witches' prophecies come true for them.

346/358 Prophecy
289/361 Treachery

354 5 5 49 'I 'gin to be aweary . . .'
Macbeth has no further interest in time. It has defeated him and he awaits death.

350/355 Macbeth
350/0   Time

355 5 5 51 'Ring the alarum bell!'
Our first knowledge of Macbeth was when we heard of him in the 'hurlyburly' of battle before he 'borrowed' the robes of Duncan. Now he throws off the mantle, reverts to the man of action and awaits the coming storm. The Macbeth whom we heard the Captain describe at the start of the play has returned. From here on, most of the play's action is accompanied by images of storms, loud noises and the roar of battle.

341/0	Clothing
354/356	Macbeth
348/356	Storm

356 5 6 9 'Make all our trumpets speak . . .'
How appropriate do you think it is that blood and noise herald the re-entry of the Thane of Glamis?

355/357	Macbeth
355/0	Storm

357 5 6 11 'They have tied me to a stake, . . .'
Macbeth compares himself to a helpless animal. He is no longer an eagle or a lion. Fate has made him powerless.

288/0	Animals
356/358	Macbeth

358 5 6 22 'But swords I smile at, . . .'
Macbeth clings to the last charm which stands between him and destruction.

357/359	Macbeth
353/361	Prophecy

359 5 6 44 'But get thee back; . . .'
Macbeth does not want to kill Macduff. Why not?

358/360	Macbeth
318/360	Macduff

360 5 6 54 'And let the angel whom thou . . .'
Time seems to laugh at Macbeth. Macduff was taken from his mother's womb early. He was a Caesarean baby therefore his mother did not bear him in the usual way. Macbeth sees that this prophecy of the Witches was also a trap.

359/363	Macbeth
359/0	Macduff

361 5 6 56 'Accursèd be that tongue that . . .'
Macbeth has now lost any trust that he had in the Witches' prophecies. Banquo was right about them. Interestingly, the image of Macduff being 'untimely ripped' from his mother's womb also recalls an image that Macbeth used at the start of the play. Can you recall this echo? (Hint: look at his speech at the start of the seventh scene in Act 1.) The image of children as agents of retribution runs through the play.

358/0	Prophecy
353/0	Treachery

362 5 6 58 'And be these juggling fiends . . .'
Has fate destroyed Macbeth, or was it the forces of evil, or was it his ambition? Can you decide where the blame should lie for his final situation? Consider whether the Witches did keep only the 'word' of their promises to Macbeth, and betray what he thought they meant. Does that make them innocent of his destruction?

256/363	Ambition
351/0	Fate

363 5 6 64 'We'll have thee, as our . . .'
How rare a 'monster' is Macbeth? Is he so rare that you cannot think of a modern example?

362/0	Ambition
360/364	Macbeth

364 5 6 66 'I will not yield . . .'

Macbeth meets his fate. 'Nothing in his life became him like the leaving it'. Where in the play have you heard this? (Hint: look at Act 1, scene 4.) Does it apply here? If it does, what implications has this for our understanding of the play?

363/366   Macbeth

---

365 5 6 78 'Your son, my lord, has paid . . .'

The final words of Ross are about the death of a young man, a hero fighting in a just cause: a man such as Macbeth used to be.

307/367   Loyalty
331/0   Ross

Seyward was Earl of Northumberland and commander of the British army. In Act 5 Menteth calls him Malcolm's uncle, although according to Holinshed he was Duncan's father-in-law, not his brother-in-law. Shakespeare may have changed the relationship because he made Duncan much older than the actual historical king would have been. Both Seyward and his son are depicted as noble, loyal soldiers of the Crown. This is why the father is so concerned for the manner of this son's death – 'Had he his hurts before?'. He must have died bravely, facing the enemy, because his wounds were not in his back – where they would have been if he had been running away.

---

366 5 6 93 'Hail, King! For so thou art.'

The rightful King is now to be enthroned. Order has returned to the State, and the time, in all senses, is free. Taken literally, the country is free of Macbeth; in the poetic sense time and the natural order are in no further danger of corruption by Macbeth.

364/369   Macbeth
332/370   Order

---

367 5 6 100 'Before we reckon with . . .'

Malcolm, like his father Duncan, shows generosity to those who are loyal to him. But his emphasis on doing things carefully, at the proper 'time, and place' suggests that he will be less easily misled than his father.

365/0   Loyalty
313/370   Malcolm

In Anglo-Saxon England an Earl was a royal governor of any of the large divisions of the Kingdom, such as Cumberland or Northumberland. The word derives from the Old English 'Earl', related to the Norse 'jarl' (chieftain) and the Old Saxon 'erl' (man).

---

368 5 6 104 'Which would be planted newly . . .'

The 'planting' image returns in its original form. The diseased crop has been weeded out and new seeds, planted at the best time, will flourish.

344/0   Growth

---

369 5 6 108 'Of this dead butcher . . .'

How accurate a judgment is this comment? Duncan was their first victim, but who or what really suffered and what was the real nature of the crime?

342/0   Lady Macbeth
366/0   Macbeth
347/370   Aspects
        of style

What is your opinion now of Macbeth? On the one hand we can see him as a person who is suspicious of everyone, haunted by whispers, words and sudden sounds. Another view of him might show us a terrified man trying to escape from his own conscience. Some people see Macbeth as a brave soldier who was also a moral coward. Think about which of these points of view you most agree with. How do you think Macbeth was seen by Banquo, Lady Macbeth, or Macduff?

Do you think this is a good ending to the play? You might feel pleased that virtue has triumphed, or sorry at the waste of a noble soldier. Both reactions are equally 'correct'. That is why the play is a tragedy. What could be said in defence of Macbeth's behaviour? Think about whether we could ever excuse the way he deliberately embraced evil. You might feel that Macbeth was, at heart, a loyal and heroic soldier. If you do, why is is that as soon as we meet him we see that his virtues have already been corrupted?

---

370   5 6 112 'We will perform in measure, . . .'
The virtuous Malcolm, though he has firm plans to consolidate the peace, will not attempt to overrule the natural order, but will put his plans into effect, with God's help, at the right time.

The end of the play is a mirror image of its start. Evil has been destroyed by good, but only by the forces of good adopting the methods of evil. In his book *Basilicon Doron*, a manual of kingship which he wrote for his son, James I argued that once someone had been accepted as King he could not be lawfully deposed. So Macbeth has been deposed illegally.

Another irony lies in the description of Macbeth as a butcher, for it is *his* body which is butchered by the hacking off of his head.

To what extent is the end of the play a signal that another destructive cycle has begun? Or can we accept that, as Macbeth stated in Act 1, scene 7 'this blow might be the be-all and the end-all!'?

367/0   Malcolm
366/0   Order
369/0   Aspects
            of style

Characters in the play

Banquo

The loyal and honourable Banquo is with Macbeth when he first meets the Witches, but their reactions are entirely different. He is deeply suspicious of their powers, and although their prophecy to him disturbs his dreams, he looks to divine help to fight their evil. After Duncan's death, Macbeth cannot bear the presence of this wise and moral man; but, after his own death, Banquo haunts Macbeth for the rest of his life, with the constant reminder that the descendants of this virtuous man will eventually be rightful kings.

Duncan

Duncan is shown as deeply appreciative of loyalty, full of dignity and virtue. Macbeth understands this well. He is perhaps too generous; his 'More is thy due' to Macbeth is taken too literally by Macbeth! He is perhaps also too trusting – of both the Thanes of Cawdor – but his kingly qualities show up Macbeth's dismal pretence for what it is; and at the end of the play the thoughtful Malcolm is encouraged to add the quality of caution to his already admirable character.

Fleance

This is a character whom we see only briefly, but whose existence haunts Macbeth, since it is through his line that the succession to the throne has been prophesied. His relationship with his father seems to be an affectionate one (like that of Lady Macduff and her son) and highlights the humanity of Banquo compared with Macbeth. Even as he is dying, Banquo's only thought is for the safety of his son.

Lennox and Ross

Lennox and Ross are not just the message-bearers and narrators they may appear at first glance. A little study shows us Shakespeare's skill in portraying them as examples of the trusting, uncomplicated, non-political majority of people. They transfer their allegiance from the murdered Duncan to Macbeth because he appears to be the legitimate king, and they appear to believe the lies told about Duncan's death, although they seem vaguely aware that something is wrong. They reflect the growing unease at Macbeth's court, and finally defect when his crimes become too bad. They will not serve a tyrant.

Macbeth

Macbeth's character develops as the play progresses. In the beginning he is a successful general, a man of action, described as noble, valiant, and worthy. We learn that he is ambitious, and prepared to accept ill-gotten gains as long as his own conscience is clear. His fatal weakness, then, is that he thinks ends and means can be separated. Lady Macbeth plays on his weakness and persuades him to murder Duncan. But as a villain, he has a fatal weakness – too much imagination. Fear and suspicion drive him into a tyrannous blood-bath. 'Noble Macbeth' becomes 'this dead butcher'.

Lady Macbeth

It is tempting to dismiss Lady Macbeth as Macbeth's evil inspiration: Adam's Eve, a traditional villainess. But Shakespeare did not insult his audience with cardboard characters. True, she is ambitious, single-minded and apparently unscrupulous, but one must have some pity for her ultimately damning failings – a lack both of imagination and of knowledge of human nature. She tries to deny her own conscience, but when her suppressed feelings burst out they completely overwhelm her and she is punished with madness.

Macduff

Macduff is the first character, apart from Banquo (who has better evidence), to have suspicions about Duncan's murder and of Macbeth's fitness to be king. He is a shrewd man, yet he has not foreseen the web of intrigue woven by Macbeth and is perhaps too honest and chivalrous himself to imagine the possibility of the callous murder of his wife and children after he has gone to England for help. In his conversation with Malcolm we come to appreciate his honourable and loyal nature; the terrible anguish he feels at his family's massacre is Macbeth's doom, exactly as the Witches prophesied.

Lady Macduff

We only meet Lady Macduff a short time before her murder but her character is quickly outlined; she is a loving wife and mother, loyal to her husband, although shrewd enough to see the danger he has left her in, and defiant towards the thugs who are about to murder her. Her dramatic importance is in the contrast of her character with Lady Macbeth's, and in the sympathy she arouses so that we appreciate the full horror of Macbeth's callousness. It is her death which finally unhinges Lady Macbeth and leads to the killing of Macbeth.

Malcolm

Malcolm, like his father, values the loyalty and bravery of Banquo and Macbeth, but is much more than a mirror image of Duncan. He is quick to sense the danger after his father's death, and has become shrewd and self-possessed by the time we meet him next, in conversation with Macduff in London. It is he who has the intelligence to use the trees of Birnam Wood as camouflage, who organizes the final assault on Dunsinane, and whose last speech in the play, of gratitude, hope and faith, convinces the audience that Scotland once again has a virtuous king.

Porter

The porter-at-the-gate-of-hell routine was an old favourite in the theatre, but Shakespeare used it cleverly for his own dramatic purpose. His Porter is a welcome relief from the heavy drama of the previous scenes; his allusions to candidates for hell not only mirror contemporary scapegoats but cunningly parallel themes of the play itself. The vulgar, music-hall humour of his dialogue with Macduff would be sure to amuse and keep the attention of the more down-to-earth members of the audience.

Witches

The Witches are the embodiment of disorder, darkness and chaos, in fact 'living' images of the evil that may tempt men's minds. Banquo senses that they are evil but Macbeth is tempted because they seem to voice his own thoughts, and Lady Macbeth is only too ready to add her voice to theirs. The Witches never lie, but in the paradoxical statements of their Apparitions, Macbeth only hears what he wants to hear. Too late he realizes that they are not interested in him but only in the triumph of evil over goodness. His final 'confusion' is what they wanted.

What happens in each act

Act One

We meet Macbeth at the height of his reputation as a military leader, a man heaped with honours by the King. These honours have been prophesied by three Witches whom he has met, which encourage him to trust their further prophecy – that he will himself become King. His wife persuades him to make the prophecy come true by murdering King Duncan.

Scene 1   The Witches appear and agree to meet again on the heath before sunset, where they say they will find Macbeth.

Scene 2   The wounded Captain reports to King Duncan on the state of the battle. Macbeth has killed Macdonwald and put his head on the battlements. The enemy army take to their boats but attack again, strengthened by reinforcements from the 'Norweyan Lord'. The ensuing battle is exceedingly bloody, and Macbeth and Banquo fight with frightening power. The Captain has to be taken away for medical attention. Ross enters and reports from Fife that the treacherous Thane of Cawdor has been helping the Norwegian king, but that they won the battle nevertheless. Sweno, the King of Norway, craves a truce. Duncan condemns the Thane of Cawdor to death and gives his title to Macbeth.

Scene 3   The first Witch tells the others about a sailor and his wife that she is persecuting. Macbeth and Banquo enter and the Witches hail Macbeth as Thane of Glamis, Thane of Cawdor and 'king hereafter'. They also hail Banquo as 'lesser' and 'greater' than Macbeth, 'not so happy' but also 'happier' than he, and the father of kings. Macbeth commands them to stay and tell them more but they vanish. Ross and Angus arrive with the news that the King has made Macbeth Thane of Cawdor. Macbeth wonders privately about the implications for his future.

Scene 4   Duncan hears that the original Thane of Cawdor has been executed and that he died with honour. The King greets Macbeth and Banquo, who thank him for his gratitude for their victory in battle. Duncan announces that his son, Malcolm, is to be named as the Prince of Cumberland. Duncan also says that he will go next to stay at Macbeth's castle in Inverness. Macbeth resolves to 'o'erleap' the problem of Malcolm and tells the audience that he has 'black and deep desires'.

Scene 5   Lady Macbeth reads a letter from Macbeth in which he tells her of the events so far, and that Duncan is coming to stay with them. She decides to urge him to follow his ambition. She vows to murder Duncan whilst he is with them, and she tells Macbeth this when he arrives.

Scene 6   Duncan arrives at Macbeth's castle, with his court. Banquo and Duncan admire the lovely surroundings of the castle and its pleasant atmosphere. Lady Macbeth welcomes them all.

Scene 7   Macbeth agonizes with himself about whether or not he should kill Duncan. Lady Macbeth enters and he says that he has decided to 'proceed no further'. Lady Macbeth is scornful of her husband and accuses him of cowardice. She tells him of her plan to kill Duncan and put the blame on his guards, whose evening drink she will drug. Macbeth becomes enthusiastic again and decides to go ahead with the murder after all.

Act Two

Although nagged by doubts, Macbeth murders the King, who is a guest in his castle, and his grooms are smeared with his blood. Suspicion falls on the grooms but the King's son, Malcolm, is dubious and flees to England. Macduff is equally suspicious, and hearing that Macbeth is to be crowned King, returns to his castle at Fife.

Scene 1   Banquo and Fleance are on night-guard when Macbeth enters. Macbeth and Banquo agree to discuss the matter of the Witches some other time. Banquo and Fleance exit. Macbeth tells his servant to ask Lady Macbeth to ring the bell when his evening drink is ready. He is left alone and sees the vision of the dagger. The bell rings and Macbeth exits to go and kill Duncan.

Scene 2   Lady Macbeth enters alone and tells the audience that Macbeth is doing the evil deed. She says that she left the daggers ready for Macbeth, and that were it not for the fact that the sleeping Duncan reminded her of her father she would have killed him herself. Macbeth enters with two bloodstained daggers, having committed the murder. He says that Duncan's guards had a troubled sleep and awoke, whilst he was hiding there, to say their prayers before settling down again. He could not say 'Amen' with them at the end of the prayers. He becomes distraught but Lady Macbeth tells him not to be foolish. They hear knocking at the castle's south entry and they retire to put on their nightgowns.

Scene 3   The Porter answers the door, very slowly and with much comical grumbling. He lets in Macduff and Lennox who exchange friendly banter with him for being so slow. Macbeth enters and Macduff says that they are here to call on Duncan as the King requested. Macduff goes to wake the King. Lennox says that the night has been very 'unruly'. Macduff returns with the news of the murder. Macbeth goes with Lennox to see the body. The alarm bell is rung. Everyone is woken up and gathers to discuss the deed. Macbeth says that he killed the guards in his fury, because he thought they had committed the murder. Lady Macbeth faints. Banquo says that everyone should get dressed, then return to investigate the murder. All agree and depart, except Duncan's sons Malcolm and Donalbain, who agree to flee for their lives to England and Ireland, respectively.

Scene 4   Ross meets an Old Man. They discuss events so far. Macduff enters with the news that Macbeth is named as the new King and has gone to Scone to be crowned. Duncan's body has been taken to Colmekill. Macduff says he is not going to Scone, he is going to Fife.

Act Three

Time has passed and Macbeth's court is uneasy. Macbeth fears Banquo, his friend, who heard the Witches' prophecies. These included one to Banquo, that his descendants would inherit the crown. Macbeth cleverly arranges for Banquo to be murdered, but that night he is haunted by Banquo's ghost, which completely unnerves him. However he cannot undo his deeds; he can only go on.

Scene 1   Banquo muses to himself about his suspicions of Macbeth. Macbeth (as King) enters with his wife and they remind Banquo not to miss the feast that night. Banquo says that he is going riding that afternoon with Fleance, his son, but that he will be back in time. Macbeth has a secret meeting with the murderers, when he tells them that Banquo has been responsible for their poor fortune in the world. They agree to murder him for Macbeth.

Scene 2   Lady Macbeth is tormented with fears for their future, as is her husband. They do not feel safe but Macbeth says they soon will, although he will not tell his wife about his plot to murder Banquo and Fleance.

Scene 3   The murderers attack Banquo and Fleance. Banquo is killed but Fleance escapes.

Scene 4   Macbeth and Lady Macbeth welcome their guests to the banquet. The First Murderer arrives and gives Macbeth the news about Banquo and Fleance. Macbeth returns to the banquet and the ghost of Banquo appears. Macbeth becomes highly agitated. Lady

Macbeth makes the excuse that Macbeth often has sudden attacks like this and has done since he was young. She says he will be fine again in a moment. The ghost appears again to Macbeth. His agitation increases and Lady Macbeth has to end the feast and send everyone home. Macbeth says he will return tomorrow to the Witches, to learn the future.

Scene 5   Hecat chastises the Witches for meddling with Macbeth and for leaving her out. She forgives them and says that they will meet Macbeth in the morning, at the pit of Acheron.

Scene 6   Lennox talks to another (unnamed) Lord and recounts Macbeth's part in the deeds so far. They say that Macduff has gone to the English court to help Malcolm raise an army. They hope to get the English King to encourage Seyward, the Earl of Northumberland, to help them overthrow Macbeth.

Act Four

Macbeth seeks out the Witches who seem to tell him he is unconquerable, but that Banquo's heirs will, indeed, sit on the throne. Macbeth is horrified to hear that Macduff has gone to England and has his family murdered. When Macduff hears of this it confirms his plan to join Malcolm, and the army which he has raised in England, to return to Scotland and kill Macbeth.

Scene 1   The Witches concoct their charm around the cauldron. Macbeth enters and demands to know the future. He is shown four Apparitions: a bodiless head wearing armour; a bloody child; a child with a tree in his hand and a crown on his head. He is told to beware of Macduff, that no man born of woman can defeat him and that he cannot be vanquished until Birnam Wood marches against him to Dunsinane Hill. Macbeth takes these as impossible events and decides that he is therefore impregnable as King. He demands to know whether Banquo's sons will ever be Kings. The fourth Apparition appears. It is a line of kings with Banquo at the end, pointing at them as though they were his. The Witches vanish. Macbeth hears from Lennox that Macduff has fled to England. He decides to raid Macduff's castle in Fife and murder all his family.

Scene 2   Macduff's castle is attacked and his wife and children murdered.

Scene 3   Malcolm and Macduff bemoan the sad state of Scotland under Macbeth's rule. Malcolm tests Macduff's loyalty to the Crown by saying that he has many vices and will be an evil king. Macduff eventually rebels at this, tells Malcolm he is not fit to live, and makes to leave. Malcolm says he was only testing his loyalty and that Macduff's virtues have cured him of all his vices, and that he will be a good king. Macduff is confused! Ross arrives with the news about the raid on Macduff's castle. Macduff vows that he will kill Macbeth.

Act Five

Malcolm and Macduff meet all the leading noblemen who have defected from Macbeth. Macbeth receives the news that his wife, who had become demented with guilt, is dead. His castle is easily taken as more and more of his men desert. Macbeth is desperate but still thinks he cannot be killed. However, the Witches have tricked him. He can be killed by Macduff. Macbeth goes into his last battle like the fearless soldier of the first Act; but Macduff kills him, and Malcolm is hailed as the new King of Scotland.

Scene 1   A doctor and one of Lady Macbeth's ladies-in-waiting discuss the health of Lady Macbeth, who enters walking in her sleep. She washes her hands and gives away secrets about the murders of Duncan and Macduff's wife. The doctor fears that he has no cure for her illness.

Scene 2   Menteth, Cathness, Angus and Lennox arrive with soldiers. They are on their way to Birnam to meet Malcolm, Seyward and Macduff, who have brought an army with them from England.

Scene 3   A servant enters to tell Macbeth that the English army is coming. Macbeth calls for his armour and asks the doctor how Lady Macbeth is. The doctor says that she has a troubled mind. Macbeth repeats the Apparition's prophecy about him being safe until Birnam Wood comes to Dunsinane.

Scene 4   The English army meets up with the Scottish Lords at Birnam Wood. Malcolm tells the men to cut branches to hide behind so that Macbeth will not know how strong their army is.

Scene 5   Seyton enters to tell Macbeth that his wife has died. A messenger arrives to say that Birnam Wood seems to be moving towards them and is within three miles of the castle. Macbeth vows to fight anyway.

Scene 6   The English army reaches the castle and the battle begins. Macbeth kills Seyward's son. Macduff looks for Macbeth. Macbeth's castle is easily conquered because his own men have turned and fought on the side of the English. Macduff and Macbeth meet and fight. Macduff reveals that his was a Caesarean birth and therefore he is not strictly 'born of woman'. Macbeth refuses to fight until Macduff calls him a coward. They fight and Macbeth is killed. Malcolm says that Scotland has been rescued from evil and invites everyone to come and see him crowned King at Scone.

Coursework and preparing for the examination

If you wish to gain a certificate in English literature then there is no substitute for studying the text/s on which you are to be examined. If you cannot be bothered to do that, then neither this guide nor any other will be of use to you.

Here we give advice on studying the text, writing a good essay, producing coursework, and sitting the examination. However, if you meet problems you should ask your teacher for help.

Studying the text

No, not just read – study. You must read your text at least twice. Do not dismiss it if you find a first reading difficult or uninteresting. Approach the text with an open mind and you will often find a second reading more enjoyable. When you become a more experienced reader enjoyment usually follows from a close study of the text, when you begin to appreciate both what the author is saying and the skill with which it is said.

Having read the text, you must now study it. We restrict our remarks here to novels and plays, though much of what is said can also be applied to poetry.

1 You will know in full detail all the major incidents in your text, **why**, **where** and **when** they happen, **who** is involved, **what** leads up to them and what follows.

2 You must show that you have an **understanding of the story**, the **characters**, and the **main ideas** which the author is exploring.

3 In a play you must know what happens in each act, and more specifically the organization of the scene structure – how one follows from and builds upon another. Dialogue in both plays and novels is crucial. You must have a detailed knowledge of the major dialogues and soliloquies and the part they play in the development of plot, and the development and drawing of character.

4 When you write about a novel you will not normally be expected to quote or to refer to specific lines but references to incidents and characters must be given, and they must be accurate and specific.

5 In writing about a play you will be expected both to paraphrase dialogue and quote specific lines, always provided, of course, that they are actually contributing something to your essay!

To gain full marks in coursework and/or in an examination you will also be expected to show your own reaction to, and appreciation of, the text studied. The teacher or examiner always welcomes those essays which demonstrate the student's own thoughtful response to the text. Indeed, questions often specify such a requirement, so do participate in those classroom discussions, the debates, class dramatizations of all or selected parts of your text, and the many other activities which enable a class to share and grow in their understanding and feeling for literature.

Making notes

A half-hearted reading of your text, or watching the 'film of the book' will not give you the necessary knowledge to meet the above demands.

As you study the text jot down sequences of events; quotations of note; which events precede and follow the part you are studying; the characters involved; what the part being studied contributes to the plot and your understanding of character and ideas.

Write single words, phrases and short sentences which can be quickly reviewed and which will help you to gain a clear picture of the incident being studied. Make your notes neat and orderly, with headings to indicate chapter, scene, page, incident, character, etc, so that you can quickly find the relevant notes or part of the text when revising.

Writing the essay

Good essays are like good books, in miniature; they are thought about, planned, logically structured, paragraphed, have a clearly defined pattern and development of thought, and are presented clearly – and with neat writing! All of this will be to no avail if the tools you use, i.e. words, and the skill with which you put them together to form your sentences and paragraphs are severely limited.

How good is your general and literary vocabulary? Do you understand and can you make appropriate use of such terms as 'soliloquy', 'character', 'plot', 'mood', 'dramatically effective', 'comedy', 'allusion', 'humour', 'imagery', 'irony', 'paradox', 'anti-climax', 'tragedy'? These are all words which examiners have commented on as being misunderstood by students.

Do you understand 'metaphor', 'simile', 'alliteration'? Can you say what their effect is on you, the reader, and how they enable the author to express himself more effectively than by the use of a different literary device? If you cannot, you are employing your time ineffectively by using them.

You are writing an English literature essay and your writing should be literate and appropriate. Slang, colloquialisms and careless use of words are not tolerated in such essays.

Essays for coursework

The exact number of essays you will have to produce and their length will vary; it depends upon the requirements of the examination board whose course you are following, and whether you will be judged solely on coursework or on a mixture of coursework and examination.

As a guide, however your course is structured, you will be required to provide a folder containing at least ten essays, and from that folder approximately five will be selected for moderation purposes. Of those essays, one will normally have been done in class-time under conditions similar to those of an examination. The essays must cover the complete range of course requirements and be the unaided work of the student. One board specifies that these pieces of continuous writing should be a minimum of 400 words long, and another, a minimum of 500 words long. Ensure that you know what is required for your course, and do not aim for the minimum amount – write a full essay then prune it down if necessary.

Do take care over the presentation of your final folder of coursework. There are many devices on the market which will enable you to bind your work neatly, and in such a way that you can easily insert new pieces. Include a 'Contents' page and a front and back cover to keep your work clean. Ring binders are unsuitable items to hand in for **final** assessment purposes as they are much too bulky.

What sort of coursework essays will you be set? All boards lay down criteria similar to the following for the range of student response to literature that the coursework must cover.

Work must demonstrate that the student:

1 shows an understanding not only of surface meaning but also of a deeper awareness of themes and attitudes;

2 recognizes and appreciates ways in which authors use language;

3 recognizes and appreciates ways in which writers achieve their effects, particularly in how the work is structured and its characterization;

4 can write imaginatively in exploring and developing ideas so as to communicate a sensitive and informed personal response to what is read.

Much of what is said in the section **Writing essays in an examination** (below) is relevant here, but for coursework essays you have the advantage of plenty of time to prepare your work – so take advantage of it.

There is no substitute for arguing, discussing and talking about a question on a particular text or theme. Your teacher should give you plenty of opportunity for this in the classroom. Listening to what others say about a subject often opens up for you new ways to look at and respond to it. The same can be said for reading about a topic. Be careful not to copy down slavishly what others say and write. Jot down notes then go away and think about what you have heard, read and written. Make more notes of your own and then start to clarify your own thoughts, feelings and emotions on the subject about which you are writing. Most students make the mistake of doing their coursework essays in a rush – you have time so use it.

Take a great deal of care in planning your work. From all your notes, write a rough draft and then start the task of really perfecting it.

1 Look at your arrangement of paragraphs, is there a logical development of thought or argument? Do the paragraphs need rearranging in order? Does the first or last sentence of any paragraph need redrafting in order to provide a sensible link with the preceding or next paragraph?

2 Look at the pattern of sentences within each paragraph. Are your thoughts and ideas clearly developed and expressed? Have you used any quotations, paraphrases, or references to incidents to support your opinions and ideas? Are those references relevant and apt, or just 'padding'?

3 Look at the words you have used. Try to avoid repeating words in close proximity one to another. Are the words you have used to comment on the text being studied the most appropriate and effective, or just the first ones you thought of?

4 Check your spelling and punctuation.

5 Now write a final draft, the quality of which should reflect the above considerations.

Writing essays in an examination
Read the question. Identify the key words and phrases. Write them down, and as they are dealt with in your essay plan, tick them off.

Plan your essay. Spend about five minutes jotting down ideas; organize your thoughts and ideas into a logical and developing order – a structure is essential to the production of a good essay. Remember, brief, essential notes only!

Write your essay
How long should it be? There is no magic length. What you must do is answer the question set, fully and sensitively in the time allowed. You will probably have about forty minutes to answer an essay question, and within that time you should produce an essay between roughly 350 and 500 words in length. Very short answers will not do justice to the question, very long answers will probably contain much irrelevant information and waste time that should be spent on the next answer.

How much quotation? Use only that which is apt and contributes to the clarity and quality of your answer. No examiner will be impressed by 'padding'.

What will the examiners be looking for in an essay?
1 An answer to the question set, and not a prepared answer to another, albeit slightly similar question done in class.

2 A well-planned, logically structured and paragraphed essay with a beginning, middle and end.

3 Accurate references to plot, character, theme, as required by the question.

4 Appropriate, brief, and if needed, frequent quotation and references to support and demonstrate the comments that you are making in your essay.

5 Evidence that reading the text has prompted in you a personal response to it, as well as some judgment and appreciation of its literary merit.

How do you prepare to do this?

1 During your course you should write between three to five essays on each text.

2 Make good use of class discussion etc, as mentioned in a previous paragraph on page 73.

3 Try to see a live performance of a play. It may help to see a film of a play or book, though be aware that directors sometimes leave out episodes, change their order, or worse, add episodes that are not in the original – so be very careful. In the end, there is no substitute for **reading and studying** the text!

Try the following exercises without referring to any notes or text.

1 Pick a character from your text.

2 Make a list of his/her qualities – both positive and negative ones, or aspects that you cannot quite define. Jot down single words to describe each quality. If you do not know the word you want, use a thesaurus, but use it in conjunction with a dictionary and make sure you are fully aware of the meaning of each word you use.

3 Write a short sentence which identifies one or more places in the text where you think each quality is demonstrated.

4 Jot down any brief quotation, paraphrase of conversation or outline of an incident which shows that quality.

5 Organize the list. Identify groupings which contrast the positive and negative aspects of character.

6 Write a description of that character which makes full use of the material you have just prepared.

7 What do you think of the character you have just described? How has he/she reacted to and coped with the pressures of the other characters, incidents, and the setting of the story? Has he/she changed in any way? In no more than 100 words, including 'evidence' taken from the text, write a balanced assessment of the character, and draw some conclusions.

You should be able to do the above without notes, and without the text, unless you are to take an examination which allows the use of plain texts. In plain text examinations you are allowed to take in a copy of your text. It must be without notes, either your own or the publisher's. The intention is to enable you to consult a text in the examination so as to confirm memory of detail, thus enabling a candidate to quote and refer more accurately in order to illustrate his/her views that more effectively. Examiners will expect a high standard of accurate reference, quotation and comment in a plain text examination.

Sitting the examination

You will have typically between two and five essays to write and you will have roughly 40 minutes, on average, to write each essay.

On each book you have studied, you should have a choice of doing at least one out of two or three essay titles set.

1 **Before sitting the exam**, make sure you are completely clear in your mind that you know exactly how many questions you must answer, which sections of the paper you must tackle, and how many questions you may, or must, attempt on any one book or in any one section of the paper. If you are not sure, ask your teacher.

2 **Always read the instructions** given at the top of your examination paper. They are

there to help you. Take your time, and try to relax – panicking will not help.

3 **Be very clear about timing, and organizing your time.**

(a) Know how long the examination is.
(b) Know how many questions you must do.
(c) Divide (b) into (a) to work out how long you may spend on each question. (Bear in mind that some questions may attract more marks, and should therefore take proportionately more time.)
(d) Keep an eye on the time, and do not spend more than you have allowed for any one question.
(e) If you have spare time at the end you can come back to a question and do more work on it.
(f) Do not be afraid to jot down notes as an aid to memory, but do cross them out carefully after use – a single line will do!

4 **Do not rush the decision** as to which question you are going to answer on a particular text.

(a) Study each question carefully.
(b) Be absolutely sure what each one is asking for.
(c) Make your decision as to which you will answer.

5 **Having decided which question** you will attempt:

(a) jot down the key points of the actual question – use single words or short phrases;
(b) think about how you are going to arrange your answer. Five minutes here, with some notes jotted down will pay dividends later;
(c) write your essay, and keep an eye on the time!

6 **Adopt the same approach** for all questions. Do write answers for the maximum number of questions you are told to attempt. One left out will lose its proportion of the total marks. Remember also, you will never be awarded extra marks, over and above those already allocated, if you write an extra long essay on a particular question.

7 **Do not waste time** on the following:

(a) an extra question – you will get no marks for it;
(b) worrying about how much anyone else is writing, they can't help you!
(c) relaxing at the end with time to spare – you do not have any. Work up to the very moment the invigilator tells you to stop writing. Check and recheck your work, including spelling and punctuation. Every single mark you gain helps, and that last mark might tip the balance between success and failure – the line has to be drawn somewhere.

8 **Help the examiner.**

(a) Do not use red or green pen or pencil on your paper. Examiners usually annotate your script in red and green, and if you use the same colours it will cause unnecessary confusion.
(b) Leave some space between each answer or section of an answer. This could also help you if you remember something you wish to add to your answer when you are checking it.
(c) Number your answers as instructed. If it is question 3 you are doing, do not label it 'C'.
(d) Write neatly. It will help you to communicate effectively with the examiner who is trying to read your script.

Glossary of literary terms

Mere knowledge of the words in this list or other specialist words used when studying literature is not sufficient. You must know when to use a particular term, and be able to describe what it contributes to that part of the work which is being discussed.

For example, merely to label something as being a metaphor does not help an examiner or teacher to assess your response to the work being studied. You must go on to analyse what the literary device contributes to the work. Why did the author use a metaphor at all? Why not some other literary device? What extra sense of feeling or meaning does the metaphor convey to the reader? How effective is it in supporting the author's intention? What was the author's intention, as far as you can judge, in using that metaphor?

Whenever you use a particular literary term you must do so with a purpose and that purpose usually involves an explanation and expansion upon its use. Occasionally you will simply use a literary term 'in passing', as, for example, when you refer to the 'narrator' of a story as opposed to the 'author' – they are not always the same! So please be sure that you understand both the meaning and purpose of each literary term you employ.

This list includes only those words which we feel will assist in helping you to understand the major concepts in play and novel construction. It makes no attempt to be comprehensive. These are the concepts which examiners frequently comment upon as being inadequately grasped by many students. Your teacher will no doubt expand upon this list and introduce you to other literary devices and words within the context of the particular work/s you are studying – the most useful place to experience and explore them and their uses.

Plot This is the plan or story of a play or novel. Just as a body has a skeleton to hold it together, so the plot forms the 'bare bones' of the work of literature in play or novel form. It is however, much more than this. It is arranged in time, so one of the things which encourages us to continue reading is to see what happens next. It deals with causality, that is how one event or incident causes another. It has a sequence, so that in general, we move from the beginning through to the end.

Structure The arrangement and interrelationship of parts in a play or novel are obviously bound up with the plot. An examination of how the author has structured his work will lead us to consider the function of, say, the 43 letters which are such an important part of *Pride and Prejudice*. We would consider the arrangement of the time-sequence in *Wuthering Heights* with its 'flashbacks' and their association with the different narrators of the story. In a play we would look at the scene divisions and how different events are placed in a relationship so as to produce a particular effect; where soliloquies occur so as to inform the audience of a character's innermost emotions and feelings. Do be aware that great works of fiction are not just simply thrown together by their authors. We study a work in detail, admiring its parts and the intricacies of its structure. The reason for a work's greatness has to do with the genius of its author and the care of its construction. Ultimately, though, we do well to remember that it is the work as a whole that we have to judge, not just the parts which make up that whole.

Narrator | A narrator tells or relates a story. In *Wuthering Heights* various characters take on the task of narrating the events of the story: Cathy, Heathcliff, etc, as well as being, at other times, central characters taking their part in the story. Sometimes the author will be there, as it were, in person, relating and explaining events. The method adopted in telling the story relates very closely to style and structure.

Style | The manner in which something is expressed or performed, considered as separate from its intrinsic content or meaning. It might well be that a lyrical, almost poetical style will be used, for example concentrating on the beauties and contrasts of the natural world as a foil to the narration of the story and creating emotions in the reader which serve to heighten reactions to the events being played out on the page. It might be that the author uses a terse, almost staccato approach to the conveyance of his story. There is no simple route to grasping the variations of style which are to be found between different authors or indeed within one novel. The surest way to appreciate this difference is to read widely and thoughtfully and to analyse and appreciate the various strategies which an author uses to command our attention.

Character | A person represented in a play or story. However, the word also refers to the combination of traits and qualities distinguishing the individual nature of a person or thing. Thus, a characteristic is one such distinguishing quality: in *Pride and Prejudice*, the pride and prejudices of various characters are central to the novel, and these characteristics which are associated with Mr Darcy, Elizabeth, and Lady Catherine in that novel, enable us to begin assessing how a character is reacting to the surrounding events and people. Equally, the lack of a particular trait or characteristic can also tell us much about a character.

Character development | In *Pride and Prejudice*, the extent to which Darcy's pride, or Elizabeth's prejudice is altered, the recognition by those characters of such change, and the events of the novel which bring about the changes are central to any exploration of how a character develops, for better or worse.

Irony | This is normally taken to be the humorous or mildly sarcastic use of words to imply the opposite of what they say. It also refers to situations and events and thus you will come across references such as prophetic, tragic, and dramatic irony.

Dramatic irony | This occurs when the implications of a situation or speech are understood by the audience but not by all or some of the characters in the play or novel. We also class as ironic words spoken innocently but which a later event proves either to have been mistaken or to have prophesied that event. When we read in the play *Macbeth*:

> *Macbeth*
> Tonight we hold a solemn supper, sir,
> And I'll request your presence.

> *Banquo*
> Let your highness
> Command upon me, to the which my duties
> Are with a most indissoluble tie
> Forever knit.

we, as the audience, will shortly have revealed to us the irony of Macbeth's words. He does not expect Banquo to attend the supper as he plans to have Banquo murdered before the supper occurs. However, what Macbeth does not know is the prophetic irony of Banquo's response. His 'duties. . . a most indissoluble tie' will be fulfilled by his appearance at the supper as a ghost – something Macbeth certainly did not forsee or welcome, and which Banquo most certainly did not have in mind!

Tragedy | This is usually applied to a play in which the main character, usually a person of importance and outstanding personal qualities, falls to disaster through the combination of personal failing and circumstances with which he cannot deal. Such tragic happenings may also be central to a novel. In *The Mayor of Casterbridge*, flaws in Henchard's character are partly responsible for his downfall and eventual death.

In Shakespeare's plays, *Macbeth* and *Othello*, the tragic heroes from which the two plays take their names, are both highly respected and honoured men who have proven their outstanding personal qualities. Macbeth, driven on by his ambition and that of his very determined wife, kills his king. It leads to civil war in his country, to his own eventual downfall and death, and to his wife's suicide. Othello, driven to an insane jealousy by the cunning of his lieutenant, Iago, murders his own innocent wife and commits suicide.

Satire   Where topical issues, folly or evil are held up to scorn by means of ridicule and irony – the satire may be subtle or openly abusive.

In *Animal Farm*, George Orwell used the rebellion of the animals against their oppressive owner to satirize the excesses of the Russian revolution at the beginning of the 20th century. It would be a mistake, however, to see the satire as applicable only to that event. There is a much wider application of that satire to political and social happenings both before and since the Russian revolution and in all parts of the world.

Images   An image is a mental representation or picture. One that constantly recurs in *Macbeth* is clothing, sometimes through double meanings of words: 'he seems rapt withal', 'Why do you dress me in borrowed robes?', 'look how our partner's rapt', 'Like our strange garments, cleave not to their mould', 'Whiles I stood rapt in the wonder of it', 'which would be worn now in their newest gloss', 'Was the hope drunk Wherein you dressed yourself?', 'Lest our old robes sit easier than our new.', 'like a giant's robe upon a dwarfish thief'. All these images serve to highlight and comment upon aspects of Macbeth's behaviour and character. In Act 5, Macbeth the loyal soldier who was so honoured by his king at the start of the play, struggles to regain some small shred of his self-respect. Three times he calls to Seyton for his armour, and finally moves toward his destiny with the words 'Blow wind, come wrack, At least we'll die with harness on our back' – his own armour, not the borrowed robes of a king he murdered.

Do remember that knowing a list of images is not sufficient. You must be able to interpret them and comment upon the contribution they make to the story being told.

Theme   A unifying idea, image or motif, repeated or developed throughout a work.

In *Pride and Prejudice*, a major theme is marriage. During the course of the novel we are shown various views of and attitudes towards marriage. We actually witness the relationships of four different couples through their courtship, engagement and eventual marriage. Through those events and the examples presented to us in the novel of other already married couples, the author engages in a thorough exploration of the theme.

This list is necessarily short. There are whole books devoted to the explanation of literary terms. Some concepts, like style, need to be experienced and discussed in a group setting with plenty of examples in front of you. Others, such as dramatic irony, need keen observation from the student and a close knowledge of the text to appreciate their significance and existence. All such specialist terms are well worth knowing. But they should be used only if they enable you to more effectively express your knowledge and appreciation of the work being studied.

Titles in the series

Pride and Prejudice
To Kill A Mockingbird
Romeo and Juliet
The Mayor of Casterbridge
Macbeth
Far from the Madding Crowd
Animal Farm
Lord of the Flies
Great Expectations
Of Mice and Men
A Man for All Seasons
Jane Eyre